Dancing the Cows Home

Memoirs and personal histories of the people of the Upper Midwest

Eggs in the Coffee, Sheep in the Corn
My 17 Years as a Farm Wife
Marjorie Myers Douglas

Halfway Home
A Granddaughter's Biography
Mary Logue

From the Hidewood
Memories of a Dakota Neighborhood
Robert Amerson

Dancing the Cows Home

A Wisconsin Girlhood

Sara De Luca

Minnesota Historical Society Press
St. Paul

Midwest Reflections
Memoirs and personal histories of the people of the Upper Midwest

Minnesota Historical Society Press
St. Paul 55102

Manufactured in the United States of America
10 9 8 7 6 5 4 3 2 1

International Standard Book Number 0-87351-324-X (cloth)
0-87351-325-8 (paper)

∞ The paper used in this publication meets the minimum requirements of the American National Standard for Information Sciences—Permanence for Printed Library Materials, ANSI Z39.48–1984.

Library of Congress Cataloging-in-Publication Data
De Luca, Sara, 1943-
Dancing the cows home : a Wisconsin girlhood / Sara De Luca.
p. cm. — (Midwest Reflections series)
ISBN 0-87351-324-X (cloth: acid-free). — ISBN 0-87351-325-8 (pbk.: acid-free)
1. De Luca, Sara, 1943- —Childhood and youth. 2. Polk County (Wis.)—Biography. 3. Twins—Wisconsin—Polk County—Biography. 4. Farm life—Wisconsin—Polk County. I. Title. II. Series.
CT275.D32755A3 1996
977.5'17—dc20 95-42676

Some of the material in this book appeared earlier in different forms in various publications: an abbreviated version of "Dancing the Cows Home" as "Confessions of a Country Ballerina" in *Iowa Woman*, 10, no. 3 (Autumn 1990); "A Better Place" in *Acorn Whistle*, 1, no. 1 (Spring 1995), and "Sheep" in the January 1996 issue; a portion of "Early Losses" as "Funerals" in *Sidewalks*, no. 8 (Spring—Summer 1995); and a number of stories as a series of vignettes in the *Amery Free Press* in 1985 and 1986.

All photographs are from the collection of the author.

To Mama for her diligence,
to Daddy for his dreams,
to Peggy for her prayers,
to Ted and Prissy for adding balance and beauty,
and to Susie for sharing every dance.

It will be a country story—
full of the breath of cows
and the scent of hay.

George Eliot

Table of Contents

Acknowledgments

Memory is fragile and fluid. Sifted through layers of time and experience, some edges soften. Others reveal themselves with increased clarity. Disjointed happenings continue to shift and warp and seek out new connections. A writer never feels quite ready to call memory truth—and set it down.

Imperfect as they are, it is time to claim these stories as my personal truth. Other family members may have stored different impressions, assigning greater or lesser importance to the events described in this book. I am reminded of the kaleidoscopes that Peggy, Susie, and I played with. They looked identical and held the same small chips of color. But each child twisted the ring to her own liking. We created our own shapes and patterns, small universes that intrigued us and drew us down inside.

This is my own universe of childhood and adolescence, viewed in the light of middle age. I have struggled with some ill-fitting fragments and nudged them into sequences that may or may not be exactly right. I have recreated conversations, staying as true to the content as I can recall it, and included excerpts from personal letters and journal entries because the voices come through so beautifully. I have also changed a few names to protect the privacy of minor players. Heroes and comedians alike are called back with affection and gratitude.

Dancing the Cows Home has been a work in progress for many years. And it would still be dancing in my head were it not for the following people who helped me bring it to the point of publication: teachers and mentors Christina Baldwin, Carol Bly, and Lawrence Sutin; friends and critics Benj Mahle, Sharri Kinkead, Marge Barrett, and Jane McDonnell; my sister Priscilla Fjorden, for material contained in "The Blacksmith"; my sister Margaret Behling, for her recollections of "The Pickle Patch"; my brother, Ted Hellerud, for remembering "Dynamite"; my twin sister, Susan Hellerud, for stimulating, critiquing, and advising me throughout this project; my mother, Helen Hellerud, for valuing the scenes of childhood and preserving them with her Kodak; my aunt, Margaret Gorder, for family photographs and letters, lovingly preserved through many decades; my patient and supportive husband, Michael De Luca; the Minnesota Historical Society Press, particularly Jean Brookins, Ann Regan, and my skillful editor, Sally Rubinstein.

Thank you for your assistance and encouragement. Thank you for helping me to bring these stories home.

Prologue: Harvey

When I was five I fell in love with my father's name.

Harvey. Harvey Henry Hellerud.

I whispered it like a prayer. I sang it aloud. I loved its breathy beginning in the back of my throat, the way it struggled with my tongue, then tried to make me smile.

I began to call him Harvey, imitating my mother in a loving voice that tilted upward toward a note of hope and praise.

"I'm your father—call me Daddy," he said sternly, refusing to answer to his name.

"Harvey. *Harvey*."

A nurse's voice, soft but insistent, called him from a morphine sleep. I was pulled into the present: 1992, an intensive care unit in a St. Paul, Minnesota, hospital where my father was dying. He had enjoyed excellent health until the past two years when his lungs grew fibrous and brittle, starving him for oxygen. He had never smoked. His heart was young and strong at seventy-nine. The doctors marveled at his lean, well-muscled form and his endurance, only recently affected.

His retirement had been heroic. At sixty-three he took up long-distance bicycling. During the ensuing summers he traveled North America from coast to coast, exploring thirty states and three Canadian provinces. At seventy-two he circled Lake Superior, a grand route that he had wanted to repeat. Two years later he started out again but called from Thunder Bay, Ontario, exhausted, asking me to fetch him home. It was his last long-distance ride.

At the time I had simply blamed the natural aging process. Now I wondered if grain dust, rotting silage, molding hay, pesticides, and herbicides had finally brought him down, more than fifteen years after he had left the farm. The doctors would not speculate. Pulmonary fibrosis, they charted. Idiopathic. Cause unknown.

"*Harvey*. Are you awake? Sara's here."

Pneumonia would soon bring the curtain down. This final scene would be short and crucial, and I had not rehearsed my part.

My childish outburst startled both of us: "You're the best father in the world!"

The ventilator tubing gagged his speech, but I could read his anguished eyes: "No, no I'm not—I've made mistakes—I've left so much undone, so much unsaid . . ."

"I love you, Daddy. We'll take care of Mama."

He closed his eyes, releasing tears into the furrows of his weathered face.

Hours later he was in a coma, but his athletic heart pumped on. The respirator wheezed and sighed, force-feeding oxygen into the body of a man who had revered the simple ways of nature. After three agonizing days, my mother, four siblings, and I all agreed that it was time to let him go, and the machines were silenced.

A chaplain summoned us for bedside prayers. Daddy's body lay still and empty. Harvey Hellerud was gone.

I felt amazed and utterly bereft. I recognized an overwhelming bleakness that had wrenched me once before, long years ago when I was five years old. That startling summer day I watched my father climb the diving tower at Balsam Beach, extend his arms like great, strong wings, arch forward, and leap head-first at the sky, then plunge into the clear, cold lake.

"Harvey flew away!" I crowed in awe, which turned to terror as I watched and waited for my father to emerge. Finally he surfaced close to shore, where he splashed me with water and hugged away my fears.

Now, forty-four years later, he had flown beyond my reach. There would be no more joking and storytelling and philosophizing with this beloved man. I would have no chance to tell him something that felt terribly important: I had researched the origins and meaning of his name.

> *Harvey*. A warrior's name which came to England during the Norman invasion. Carnage worthy; destined for ferocious battle.

Somehow I had known that a long, long time.

All through the years I had held my childhood so close and deep. Though I had hoarded many random, sharply focused scenes, I had not viewed them broadly or explored connecting themes. Now I wanted to recall those richly textured times in sequence and discover their direction and design.

In the months that followed, I sorted photos and letters. I sifted through my memories, trying to know my father's battles; they often led me toward my own. I remembered comic skirmishes and fierce engagements, full defeats and wounding blows. I recalled some triumphs, too. Those hurting, healing stories are gathered here beneath a playful banner: *Dancing the Cows Home*.

Amery Hospital
Amery, Wisconsin
May 20, 1943

Harvey Darling,

I'm sorry we didn't have more chance to talk when you visited last night. This will have to make up for it.

I'm enclosing a list of groceries that you might get, just in case you forget what to order. Be sure to get that can opener from Irene so you can be fixing yourself some soup and beans in a hurry. If you get too hungry, go over to Irene's for your dinners. She would be glad to feed you and when you are so busy it would be better for you to get at least one warm meal a day.

Remember to fix some eggs for breakfast along with your cold cereal or you'll be famished. To boil them take the small gray or white kettle and put enough water in it to about cover the eggs or a little better. Bring water to rapid boil and put eggs in gently with a spoon so they don't crack. Let them boil for a good four minutes—1/2 minute or so longer if the eggs are real large. Remember I put the eggs in two cardboard boxes down in the basement at the foot of the stairs. You may need to order some more before I come home.

My stitches are much less sore today but my breasts have inflated like balloons since last night and bother today. I'll be able to come home by about next Tuesday or Wednesday. It can't be too soon to suit me. I suppose that could be because I miss a certain swell guy . . .

I hope you're getting along as well as the Twins and I are.

All our love to the best husband and daddy in the world—

Helen, Susan and Sara

Double or Nothing

Mama saved Dr. Cornwall's bill for her ten-day stay at Amery Hospital in May 1943. It reads:

DELIVERY OF TWINS, BREECH PRESENTATION
First Baby—$100;
Second Baby—$5

I was the five-dollar kid.

Mama liked to say it was a good thing one of us was timid. Had I forged ahead with Susie, the doctor might have grabbed one leg from each baby. That could have been disastrous. But I held back, well out of reach, and let him twist and turn and pull my squirming sister down, feet first. I followed easily, five minutes later.

My twin and I were snipped from the same pattern but made of different cloth. Susan Marie remained aggressive and stubborn. I, Sara Jane, was the cautious one, content to let my sister wade ahead through stinging nettles, dive first into the icy April water, climb the slippery silo ladder while I stood below with arms extended like a safety net.

I heard the whispered observations: "They look alike, but there's a fascinating difference. Susan is the spunky one. Sara is the calm, good-natured twin."

Helen Hellerud and three-month-old twins, Susie (left) and Sara, summer 1943

One raw spring day when we were not quite six, Susie and I ran half a mile down County Road I to the gravel pit where Daddy was loading fill for the muddy driveway. After scolding us for leaving the yard without permission, he let us ride back home atop the wagonload of gravel behind the rumbling John Deere. Halfway up the long, steep drive Susie decided to fly. "Watch me!" she yelled, flapping her arms, leaping toward the sky.

She did not fling herself high or far enough to clear the rig. Her right leg struck the wagon box, and she was thrown face down in the mud, just ahead of the rear axle. I felt a thump beneath the wheel.

"Daddy! Daddy! Stop! We ran over Susie!"

My voice blew backward on the wind. I crawled toward the front of the wagon, cupped my hands around my mouth, and screamed. The tractor shrieked louder, choking and chugging up the drive. Afraid to jump, I drilled my heels into the coarse gravel and watched my sister disappear from sight.

When we finally stopped beside the barn, I jumped down and ran to Daddy, still perched high above me on the sculptured iron seat. I gasped and pointed in a frantic pantomime.

We raced to Susie who lay limp and still beside a budding lilac bush. Daddy dropped to his knees and began picking small stones from her mouth and eyes. Her left eyelid was bleeding, and he dabbed it gently with his handkerchief, then cradled her in his arms the way I had seen him do with stillborn lambs.

Almost running, he carried Susie up the driveway to the house, elbowed his way in, and laid her on the kitchen table.

Mama and Peggy watched in stunned silence.

"Oh God—I shouldn't have carried her like that," Daddy gasped. "I don't know where that tire got her . . . "

"She's breathing," Mama whispered, leaning over Susie's face. "And I can feel a steady pulse."

Susie whimpered then, setting the world in dizzy motion.

Mama knotted her best dish towels together in a lumpy rope embroidered with fruits and flowers. Daddy tied my twin to a wide leaf from the dining-room table, taking special care with her right leg, which twisted outward just above the knee. Daddy loaded Susie and the table leaf into the back seat of the Buick Special. "She'll be all right. She'll be all right," he said, as if those hopeful words could make a miracle.

Until the accident I had never been apart from Susie for a single day, not even for an hour. After her leg was broken, I could not visit her for two long weeks. All that time I felt injured and crippled, only half alive. I wondered how singles found the strength and will to live, day after lonely day.

Eight-year-old Peggy, two-year-old Teddy, and I were "farmed out" separately to relatives so Mama could stay with Susie at Amery Hospital. Mama came to see me twice at Aunty Louise's during the ordeal, bringing me treats like sticks of Dentyne gum and half a Hershey bar that Susie had saved for me. She hugged me and reported that my twin was doing fine.

After the first visit, Aunty Louise walked Mama to the car, and from the doorway I heard fragments of their anxious talk. The traction on Susie's leg was terribly painful, Mama said. Susie—never a complainer—was screaming day and night. The leg most certainly was crooked. Tomorrow Mama would insist they call a specialist from the city. The cost was not important—they would sell another heifer—whatever it might take.

Mama's worries were well founded: new x-rays showed the broken femur overlapping. An orthopedic surgeon from St. Paul would break the bone again and pin it with a metal rod. With luck and time it might be straight and strong again.

After fifteen days Susie returned home, equipped with a pair of crutches, her right leg bound in thick white plaster, hip to ankle. She coaxed her legs to action, calling them Fling and Bum. The cast was cut away in August. Poor Bum was milky white with a puckered purple scar running eight inches down the thigh. It looked like a wilted stocking darned up carelessly with mismatched thread. I was relieved to see her legs were equal length. With practice she would walk straight again and stand as tall as me.

"Back-to-back," said Mama, leveling a book across our heads.

"Still a matched set," said Daddy.

"Close enough," Mama agreed.

We started school that fall in matching daisy-print dresses sewed from flour sacks. "These look-alikes are just for fun," said

Mama. "You won't have many. Hand-me-downs don't come in pairs, and I wouldn't dress you alike every day even if I could. People need to know that you are two girls, with different names and different personalities."

Two weeks apart had been enough. We did not want to be separate girls ever again, and we worked to minimize our differences. We kept our teachers and classmates well confused. If Miss Paulson figured out that I was wearing the red jumper and Susie was wearing the blue plaid skirt, we changed clothes in the bathroom at recess time and took each other's desks. I called my twin Sara and she called me Susie. Before long we were both called "Susie-and-Sara" or simply "Twins," and no one tried to figure who was who. We were praised identically and seldom punished. Our report cards matched, although I excelled in reading and Susie was more skillful with the scissors, clay, and finger paints. We made a dandy team.

Susie lost her upper right front tooth in reading circle, second grade. "See Dick and Jane. See baby Sally. See Spot run." The books were simple, but we read haltingly, unable to concentrate. All we could see was a gaping difference that must be rectified. Susie promised she would pull my matching tooth at noon, and I said yes, okay, although I knew it was not ready. I could barely wiggle it between my thumb and finger after working it all morning long.

After lunch the class went out to play. Susie and I went straight to the girls' bathroom. I sat on the toilet, tying a store-string around the sacrificial tooth. Susie fastened the other end to the stall door.

"Say when."

"*When!*" She jerked the door wide open, and I flew off the stool, howling with pain. Miss Paulson came running. She kept us after school for a harsh scolding.

"I'm going to have to tell your parents," she warned. "This trickery has got to stop." She entrusted me with the sealed

Susie (left) and Sara with a pailful of grass clippings, summer 1947

letter, warning that I must not withhold it.

Daddy thought it was hilarious. Mama merely frowned and said we must behave a little better for Miss Paulson who had a room full of students to manage and should not be bothered with our silly stunts.

"They're really very different," we had often heard her say. "If people would just stop making such a fuss and treat them like the individuals they are . . . "

The fuss continued—at church, family gatherings, the grocery store, and everywhere we went. "Look at those darling little twins!" Always said with great commotion, always loud enough for us to hear.

We heard that sweet refrain in April 1950, when the high school prom queen and her counselor visited our classroom to pick crown bearers for the royal court. Susie and I circled the room with our classmates, stepping to a lively piano tune.

It was a cruel game of musical chairs. One by one the queen culled the homeliest, clumsiest students from the ring with her index finger, directing them back to their desks. Soon only a dozen pretty children marched around, Susie and I among them. We knew our liabilities—pug noses and straight, wispy hair. But we had graceful bodies, bright blue eyes, and winning smiles. We also knew that double was adorable. We couldn't lose.

The queen argued with her counselor, the high school typing teacher, as we strutted past.

"They're both so *precious*," the queen insisted. "How can I possibly chose only one? They look identical!"

"You have to pick a little boy, too, remember that. And we don't need *three* crown bearers—for only two crowns," the teacher chirped in a staccato voice that sounded like a typing exercise. "Besides, they can't do everything together all their lives. They'll have to be pried apart some time."

"Quite true," Miss Paulson offered from the piano bench, dropping several measures of "March Militaire." "It might as well be now."

"Well, I'm the queen, and I want *both* of them, in matching gowns," Her Highness pouted.

Crown bearers Susie, Bobby Blattner, and Sara (left to right), Balsam Lake High School Prom, May 1950

Susie and I held a hasty conference as we rounded the west corner of the room. We would excuse these foolish teachers who didn't know the first thing about being twins. We also agreed that if only one of us was chosen, she would refuse to serve. It would have to be double or nothing.

The queen prevailed. Susie and I were selected as a unit. A freckle-faced classmate, Bobby Blattner, would escort us up the aisle.

Miss Paulson scowled. "Adorable. Well, Twins, tell your mother to start sewing. She has two outfits to finish before the fifth of May."

We could hardly wait to share the news. "Mama! Mama! Sara and I need costumes for the Prom! We're going to be bears!"

"Can you do it, Mama? Where will you get the fur?"

Mama laughed. "You're going to be *crown bearers*. That means you will carry the crowns to the king and queen. I'll make you look like princesses. You'll see."

Mama ordered yards of fabric from the Sears Roebuck catalog, a crisp white Swiss sprinkled with red dots. She turned out fairy-tale dresses with short puffed sleeves, wide sashes, and floor-length skirts, tiered and trimmed with eyelet lace. There were red T-strap sandals, too, and satin ribbons for our hair.

Mama treadled on her Singer until midnight, all week long. The gowns were ready when Prom night arrived. Susie and I were perfect princesses. Bobby looked royal in his three-piece suit and shiny shoes and bashful smile. The drab gymnasium had become a paradise: twisted blue and silver streamers concealed ducts and pipes and basketball rigging; pink star dust twinkled in the sagging sky.

Mama and Daddy sat in the bleachers beside Bobby's parents and watched us march across crepe-paper heaven beneath a galaxy of cardboard stars. They must have thought about the years ahead—our future proms, dating, driving, graduating, leaving home, and coming back as grateful guests. Susie and I would do all these things in tandem. Double or nothing.

Landscapes

Our family album contains many pictures of the two-story, white frame farmhouse that was home until my twin and I were ten. The house has tall, narrow windows, open porches, deep eaves, and a steeply pitched roof designed as a defense against the harsh Wisconsin weather. It features sharp angles and bold lines, punctuated by a single brick chimney pointing skyward and by the gutters and downspouts running toward the earth.

This is an ordinary structure, hardly worthy of a portrait. It is, in fact, an incidental backdrop in these 1940s photographs of a happy threesome—Peggy, Susie, and me—somersaulting on the lawn, making mud pies on the open porches, or perched on heaping banks of snow. Summer flatters us with lacy foliage; winter stands us capped and jacketed against the sky.

These are outdoor studies, snapped in cheerful, sunny weather by our mother, Helen Hellerud. She expanded her Eastman Kodak like a small accordion, pointing it often in our direction. She always found the advantageous angle, dodged the creeping shadows, and utilized the shifting patch of sun.

Mama preserved a smiling world for us in black and white with scalloped borders. Her aim was high and wide, sometimes dwarfing her children in favor of a generous panorama. She captured the oaks and elms, the birches and lilacs. She included swings and clotheslines. She photographed the slatted corn cribs, the low-slung sheep shed, and the Gothic-roofed barn, casting its western shadow over a twenty-horse Farmall and a spiny hay rake parked nearby. Looking east, Mama preserved a crusted manure spreader, a Model D John Deere, the iron teeth of a harrow, and the petal-shaped blades of a two-bottom plow.

My interior scenes are tighter, drawn at eye level, uncertain images of doorknobs and windowsills and the geometric patterns on a cracked linoleum floor.

Most of the furnishings are vaguely remembered shapes with scratched limbs and leaky stuffing. A few fixtures remain sharp and real, like Daddy's brown easy chair with its plump cushions and curving metal arms. And the Victrola. The tall, dark Victrola, standing in the southwest corner of the parlor.

Daddy's chair was positioned like a throne before the largest parlor window. I felt relieved when he relaxed there after evening chores.

"I guess he's not cut out for farming," Mama muttered to herself as she scrubbed pots and pans at the dry sink or swept the kitchen floor with short, swift strokes. She did not seem to know that she was talking or realize I was close enough to hear. " . . . worries constantly about the weather—wet fields—late crops—things he can't control. Gets himself so worked up and exhausted he can't even sleep . . . "

Mama and Daddy usually came in from evening milking around eight o'clock, Mama's short legs stepping quickly, Daddy following behind with a slightly pigeon-toed gait that looked tired and uncertain. Mama often took her mending basket from the cupboard and sat at the dining-room table, weaving tidy cross-hatch patterns in worn heels and toes, stretching them over her tightened fist, testing the mends for strength and sturdiness. Other nights she stood at the kitchen counter, peeling apples for a batch of pies or potatoes for tomorrow's pot of stew. Daddy sank into his easy chair. He often reached for his *Reader's Digest* and tried to read but would soon be staring blankly at the pages. His large head nodded, and he snored softly. I crept away, worried by his sweaty face and gaping mouth, not wanting to disturb his badly needed rest.

Across the room stood a gift from Daddy's parents, which neither he nor Mama found much time to enjoy—an elegant Victrola poised on curving Queen Anne legs. Double doors in front hid twelve trays of thick, grooved phonograph records. Under the heavy hinged lid lay a metal platter on a lining of grass-green felt. A sturdy metal handle protruded from the left side panel. Although Susie and I were only four—too young to manage this alone—Mama had shown us how to select a record, place it on the turntable, lower the needle, and wind the crank until an entire orchestra poured out of the music machine. But we were warned to wait for Peggy, who at age seven was able to handle the records without scratching them. Sometimes when our parents were busy in the barn and Peggy was looking after our baby brother, Teddy, we played with the Victrola. We cranked the handle recklessly until Bing Crosby chirped like a cricket, then threw him into stunned reverse and wound him slowly forward to a croaking bullfrog pitch.

One evening Susie dragged a chair alongside the Victrola and climbed up to inspect its innards. She spied a little glass cup of needles, snatched one, and carved her name into the side panel: S U S A N. She began faintly, slowly, but drew each letter larger and bolder than the last, until the N was as big as her fist. It struck through the dark varnish to the raw, white wood beneath.

I watched silently, amazed at my twin, not thinking to stop her, not knowing my separateness. I was afraid but excited by the horror of the deed. It did not occur to me that I was innocent, that I would not be punished.

Peggy was the first to discover the mischief. She was too frantic to fuss or scold. "You twins are going to get it when Daddy comes in—you'd better hide!"

It was tricky hiding in a house with few closets or cupboards. We were afraid of the damp cellar with its spiders and salamanders and would not take refuge there.

We could only wait until our parents' footsteps sounded on the back porch, wait while they removed their barn boots, coats, and caps and gloves, emptied the chaff from their overall pockets, poured dippers of fresh water into the basin, and sponged their tired hands and faces.

"Would you like a peanut butter sandwich, Harvey? Or a bowl of pudding? There's some chocolate pudding in the frig."

Mama dished up a large bowl for Daddy and a small one for herself, puzzled that her daughters all declined the treat.

Finally Daddy walked into the parlor where we waited. He sank into his soft, upholstered chair and looked around until his blue eyes came to rest on the damaged Victrola.

"*Susan,*" he said slowly. "*SUSAN!*" His voice rose dangerously. The second syllable rang high and loud, just the way Susie had scratched it on the phonograph. She stepped forward and followed him into the bedroom. The door closed behind them.

Peggy ran upstairs. Mama hesitated at the doorway, palms pressed against her forehead, then wandered aimlessly from room to room.

I huddled near the bedroom door. "Goddamn it, kid! Can't we have one nice thing around here without your wrecking it?" Daddy's furious words were followed by sharp spanking sounds that made me twist and cring with every blow. When I felt thoroughly beaten, I shut my eyes and plugged my ears but could not block the sound. Whimpering, I crouched against the wall.

Stubborn Susie would not cry, so the spanking continued. Finally Daddy locked her in the cellar with the spiders. I ran to set her free. Daddy blocked my path and ordered me to bed in a high, trembling voice.

I scrambled up the stairs. Peggy and I heard Susie pounding on the cellar door, all the way to our second-story bedroom. We crawled into bed and huddled under two thick quilts, unable to stop shivering.

At last I slept and dreamed: It was a chilly, foggy night, and I had wandered alone into the swamp that lay a quarter mile beyond the barn. I was sinking deeper with every step. I heard a harsh, tinny melody rising out of the mist, faster and louder, until it became a high-pitched wail. I was to blame for the horrible music, for I had been cranking the Victrola. When I tried to slow it down, the whole weight of my body was not enough to make a difference.

Peggy

From an early age Susie and I relished Mama's stories of our birth and infancy. She told us that Peggy, who loved the neighbor's matched set of baby boys, begged for twins when she was not yet three.

"Twins aren't so easy to come by," Daddy teased.

"How can I get some?" Peggy pleaded.

"I guess you'll have to pray."

Even then Peggy, who took her Sunday school lessons very seriously, seemed to have connections with Almighty God. Susie and I were born a few months later, pink and healthy, weighing nearly seven pounds apiece.

Mama's friends were both admiring and sympathetic.

"How are you ever going to manage, Helen, with a three-year-old barely out of diapers and now a pair of *twins?*"

Mama liked to say, "One baby takes all your time—two can't possibly do more than that."

She was mistaken. Two babies demanded all of her time and more. Peggy, who had wanted twins so badly, was deposed by a pair of howling infants who expected service night and day. Snapshots from those early years capture the dilemma clearly: Mama struggling with two squirming babies, Peggy hunkered down behind, sucking fiercely on her thumb; the twins surrounded by cooing relatives, Peggy standing in the background, smiling anxiously.

With twin babies, gardening, field work, and freshening cows all competing for Mama's time and attention, Peggy must have felt abandoned. Friends and family fussed over the darling look-alikes, nearly forgetting the pretty child they had found so precious only weeks before.

Peggy had one champion who did not desert her when the

twins arrived. I recall Grandma Hellerud only as a great warm shadow, but to Peggy she was so much more.

Our family visits to the well-kept Hellerud home in Milltown were usually hurried, combined with a trip for grocery staples, feed, or fertilizer. Grandma often asked to keep our sister overnight. Peggy would return the following day, armed with the treasures she and Grandma had created—bold finger paintings of colliding stars and swirling seas, hollyhock dolls with layered skirts of white and pink and cherry red, or a sack of large, round sugar cookies she refused to share. She did attempt to share the bedtime stories Grandma told her, chattering about a girl named Heidi and an ugly duckling who became a swan.

Grandma Hellerud died of cancer in April 1947, one month after Peggy's seventh birthday. She took our sister's childhood

Helen enjoys her reunion with Susie (left), Sara (right), and Peggy (behind Susie), following Teddy's birth in August 1946.

with her. That spring Peggy began to pray compulsively. And there was much to pray about in 1947—droughts, floods, farm price supports, the Iron Curtain, cancer, polio. She knew the world was in a fearful state; prayer was the only hope, and she would try to do her part.

Peggy was a fourth grader when Susie and I started school in August 1949. We were surprised to see that she often played alone at recess or sought us out rather than joining girls her own age. She was one of the last to be chosen for games. The playground bullies called her "Piggy" and swiped her cap or pulled her hair. When she worked her mouth from side to side, I knew she was chewing the skin inside her cheeks. Sometimes she sat at her desk throughout recess, practicing her penmanship and not coming out to play at all.

She never cried or tattled. But if Peggy acted stoic at school, she worried double time at home. She crouched by the radio listening to the evening news. When the weatherman predicted early frost, she worried that the corn might not be ripening on time. She listened intently to Lowell Thomas's reports about the conflict in Korea. Her third-grade teacher was in an iron lung at Sister Kenny Institute in Minneapolis, and Peggy cried about that, thinking she was somehow to blame. When the elm branches scratched against our window on a windy night, Peggy crawled beneath the bed and slept there on the bare wood floor.

Mama and Daddy knew some of Peggy's troubles, but they had not heard the nightly prayers. Our long prayer sessions with Peggy were a worrisome secret—quite different from the joyful worship we experienced with our parents every Sunday at Faith Lutheran Church. Susie and I knelt obediently with Peggy each night in our chilly upstairs bedroom, helping pray away her fears. Our hands must be pressed together perfectly, our fingers pointed toward the sky. Our heads must bow but must never come to rest on the bed covers. When we sagged with sleep, Peggy nudged us to attention. We did our best to mind, afraid that even a hint of rebellion might cause our fragile sister to drift beyond us like a lost balloon. We knelt patiently through all the please-blesses; on a bad news day this might take an hour or more. "Please-bless President and Mrs. Truman and everyone in Washington. Please-bless the U.S. citizens. Please-bless the Russians, too, and please, God, please don't let them drop the bomb on us. Please-bless Sister Kenny and the doctors and nurses at the Institute. . . . Please-bless my teacher and all the other cripples . . . " She droned on and on. As Peggy's prayers drew homeward we knew the job was nearly done.

"Please-bless the farmers in Polk County and dry up all the fields so they can pick the corn on time . . . " And the finish: "Please-bless-Mama-Daddy-Peggy-Susie-Sara-Teddy-and-the-sheep-and cows-and-cats-Amen."

Finally she rose, allowing us to crawl beneath the quilt. Susie dived for cover, but I felt compelled to watch Peggy's stiff, silent march toward the light switch in the hallway, just beyond our bedroom door.

I had spied on Peggy's rituals many times before. I had seen her feet form perfectly square corners in the doorway as if her every step must be true and perfect, pleasing in the Master's sight. I had watched her trace small crosses in the air above our heads before she drifted off to sleep.

I did not want to watch my sister's light-switch rites, which grew more and more elaborate, yet I could not look away. She stopped abruptly in front of the switch, backed up half a step, inched forward again, then stood still, hands held tight to her sides. Slowly she lifted her arms and began arcing her splayed hands, circling downward toward the magic switch. Suddenly the bulb winked out, leaving only a white-hot halo pulsing in the void before my startled eyes.

One night Peggy woke, hysterical, to find the Holy Ghost standing just inside our bedroom door. It was only her white bathrobe hanging there, but Peggy would not be calmed, even after I jumped up and flung the robe across her bed.

"He was here to warn us!" she screamed. "We didn't pray enough tonight!"

Neither Susie nor I thought to tell our parents. Farming gave them all the worries they could handle, and no one but God could comfort our tormented sister anyway.

That autumn Mama and Daddy took us to a gospel program in a huge canvas tent that had been erected in the center of the Balsam Village Park. They hoped the sermon would be brief. It was the music they had wanted us to hear. They had been told the choir was especially fine, and this turned out to be true. A quartet of men and women sang in four-part harmony: "Joshua Fit De Battle of Jericho, and De Walls Come Tumblin' Down." These hand-clapping spirituals were nothing like the lukewarm singing in our Lutheran church on Sunday mornings.

Part way through the program a towering, white-robed minister took the microphone and began preaching the Word. His voice wound higher and faster, and he called the sinners forward, urging them to pledge their lives to Jesus. I saw Mama and Daddy shifting in their metal chairs, whispering that it was time to leave. They were gathering up their coats when Peggy slipped past them and made a dash for salvation.

"Stop her, Harvey!" Mama said, but he wasn't fast enough. The preacher hoisted Peggy up on stage. She clung to his hand while tears streamed down her cheeks.

"Ladies and gentlemen—God will ransom this courageous child! She is ready to repent of her sins, to be washed clean by Jesus! *Dear Savior, wash her in the healing stream!* Sing with me, child, and the Lord will lift you up! Join in, everyone: 'Jesus keep me near the cross . . . There are precious fountains . . .' "

Sara, Teddy, Peggy, and Susie in 1948

Peggy closed her eyes and sobbed into the microphone as more sinners marched forward to glory.

> In the cross, in the cross,
> Be my glory ever,
> Till my ransomed soul shall find
> Rest beyond the river.

When the hymn was done our sister stumbled back to her seat, eyes glazed, a pilgrim who had traveled far and touched a radiant shore.

No one said a word in the car or in the kitchen as Mama poured mugs of hot milk, adding generous portions of butter and sugar and the usual pinch of salt. Mama and Daddy sat with Peggy between them and passed their arms around her back, not quite touching her, as if she were extremely frail.

That night I understood that my older sister was seriously wounded. How hard I had tried not to see it! I had been charged since birth with looking after my reckless twin. Now I must begin protecting Peggy, too. Just how I would accomplish that I did not know.

Miss Higgins

It was hard to imagine that our overalled and kerchiefed mother, born and raised on a dairy farm near Milltown, had ever known a city life. But we had evidence: a photo of Miss Helen Williamson, with the same fine features and shy smile as our mother but dressed in a trim suit and hat, posed at the entrance of the Medical Arts Building on Ninth and Nicollet in Minneapolis.

After leaving Milltown, she attended the Minneapolis Business College and worked at Walman Optical for nearly five years. She also studied violin at MacPhail School of Music. The lessons were "too little, and too late" for any chance of a professional career, Mama told us wistfully. She had also fallen in love with our father. In 1939 she returned to Milltown and became a farmer's wife. The violin was in the back of her closet, and the stylish clothes were boxed away in the storeroom. She did not seem to miss them, except when her Minneapolis friend, Anne Higgins, came to visit. Then Mama talked about her city years—the concerts, plays, motion pictures, and shopping trips to Dayton's Department Store.

"The skirts are so much longer this year, Helen. I've had to replace all my suits, and you know they cost a fortune now—no more three-dollar outfits like we used to find in Dayton's basement."

"Good thing I moved to the country where no one cares what I look like. I'd never be able to afford those fashions."

"Sure you would, Helen! You'd have been in charge of

Walman's accounts by now, earning forty dollars a week!"

Mama shook her head. "I do miss those concerts. Is Mitropoulos still conducting the Minneapolis Symphony? How do they sound this year?"

Mama said Anne Higgins had been like a big sister to her. We couldn't picture that. Miss Higgins was so very different from our mother. We knew she was unmarried, an "old maid." Irish Catholic, too, which was a curious thing. We had some Irish Catholic neighbors and had heard that they were always playing with beads or fighting or having babies. Miss Higgins did not seem to fit that mold at all. She was childless and prim and private, groomed accordingly with dark hair drawn back in a tight bun and wire-rimmed glasses perched midway down her long, thin nose.

Miss Higgins, wearing a tweed suit, long-sleeved blouse, silk hose, and high-heeled shoes, had arrived on the Greyhound bus. She never changed into sensible country clothes and did not venture near the barn or show the slightest interest in the crops or cattle.

"How in the world do you manage all of this?" Miss Higgins asked, surveying Mama's garden at a careful distance. She toured the spacious front yard with cautious steps, carrying a broad umbrella to shield her from the summer sun.

Miss Higgins talked about general ledgers and receivables while Mama washed and mended, cooked and cleaned, for one whole week in August 1949. When Mama picked her beans and cukes, Miss Higgins high-stepped through the vines, describing every window display along Nicollet and Hennepin Avenues.

Miss Higgins paid little attention to us kids, so we were surprised—and slightly reluctant—when she wrote a few months later and invited us girls to visit her in Minneapolis. Mama hesitated, too. Peggy was nine years old; Susie and I were only six, and we twins had never been away from home, except for an

Anne Higgins visiting the farm with Susie (left) and Sara

occasional overnight with Grandma Williamson and when Susie broke her leg.

We heard our parents discussing the unusual invitation.

"I think she's lonely, Harvey. Especially during the holidays. I just wonder if she can manage three of them—they can get pretty boisterous. And she seems so . . . delicate."

"I think they'll be just fine, Helen. They'll love the Christmas lights! Besides, you could use some quiet time, with the baby coming in January. Maybe we can send Teddy to your mother's for a few days—then you could really get a rest."

So it was settled. We would stay three days and two nights with Miss Anne Higgins in her small apartment at the Leamington Hotel.

Peggy, Susie, and I left in the early morning of December 17 with our neighbor, Jug Johnson, who had business in the city. Jug's '47 Buick was spotlessly clean until Susie vomited her sausage and scrambled eggs all over the back seat. The temperature was twenty-two below zero, too cold to roll down any windows and circulate some air. Jug, who was usually so friendly, handed back a greasy rag and growled. At sun-up he delivered us, rumpled and reeking, to the Leamington doorman and sped away in an amazing stream of traffic.

Miss Higgins, our anxious guardian, was waiting in the lobby. She smiled doubtfully, wrinkling her prominent nose. "As soon as we clean up at bit, I'll show you downtown Minneapolis—all the places that your mother used to love so well."

Until this moment my sisters and I had never known buildings more than two stories tall, except for wooden stave or concrete towers, warm and fragrant with the briny gas of rotting corn. Here were massive city silos, holding homes and shops and offices behind cold, flat walls of brick and glass and steel.

That afternoon we rode an elevator to the top of the very tallest one—the Foshay Tower—where we looked over the huge, blinking city. We were dazzled by the window displays on Nicollet Avenue and by the Salvation Army Santas jingling their bells on every busy corner. Even the traffic lights beamed holiday colors of red and green and gold. We stumbled through a revolving door into Dayton's Department Store, where Miss Higgins invited us to select Christmas gifts—"one for each of you—no sharing this time." We picked out look-alike wooden batons, red and blue striped, splashed with silver glitter—and twirled them over our heads as we walked down the crowded sidewalk. Shoppers scattered as we passed.

Miss Higgins had three lively little girls in tow and only two hands with which to tow them. I was cut adrift—so busy craning my neck to study the tall buildings that I fell behind and did not notice. When I took the hand of a woman marching beside me, she jerked away. I had latched onto a perfect stranger. Overcome with panic, I dropped my baton and stumbled forward, dodging elbows, bags, and boxes, until I spied Miss Higgins and my sisters at the traffic light. I ran to them, gasping with relief. They had not missed me.

"Don't worry about the baton," said Susie. "We'll just share this one."

Soon we were sharing something even better—our first ride on a moving stairway called an escalator. Timidly I stepped aboard and glided downward without moving my feet at all. My stomach lurched; so did my oatmeal, which landed on the rolling steps and disappeared into the works, just before I reached solid ground.

Miss Higgins steered us quickly forward, into the brisk outdoors. When I had recovered my appetite we stopped to eat at Woolworth's lunch counter. A sickening odor stung the air, making me think that several diners had thrown up on their plates.

"More vomit!" I exclaimed.

"Oh, no!" Miss Higgins said with a rare laugh. "That's a new food everyone seems to love. They call it pizza. Would you like to try it?"

None of us was feeling quite that brave. We craved Mama's pot roast and mashed potatoes, but it was not on the menu, so we asked for hamburgers instead.

After lunch we saw a real live midget scrambling up on a stool to order a sandwich. Miss Higgins would not let us stay and watch her, explaining that it was impolite to stare.

We moved on to Dayton's toy department where Miss Higgins bought me a wonderful gift to make up for the lost baton.

"It's called a kaleidoscope," she said. "It will show you a thousand patterns, like colored snowflakes. No two will ever be the same."

Peggy asked Miss Higgins to help her find a toilet, and we wound our way through aisles of handbags, slippers, jewelry, and perfumes. Dayton's had a large "powder room" with six toilet stalls, but only one was free of charge, and that door stood halfway open like an invitation. The rest were locked tight with small, silver coin boxes requiring a dime admission.

Peggy hurried toward the open stall.

"Oh, no, dear! Leave that one for the darkies!" Miss Higgins said. "Here, take this dime—I'll show you how it works."

It seemed an incredible thing, paying to go to the toilet, especially when there was a choice of going free. I guessed there was a complicated reason, something shameful that I should not ask about.

"How about the twins? I have plenty of coins."

"No thanks. We'll wait awhile."

Miss Higgins admitted she was tired; she summoned a cab that took us back to the hotel, and we spent the rest of the afternoon in her apartment at the Leamington Hotel. Not counting the tiny bathroom, it was one all-purpose room with a bed called Murphy that folded down from the wall and a miniature kitchen hidden behind folding doors. It was not as grand as I had imagined, but the high-rise view was wonderful. Cars crept along the street; people moved in tune with the traffic lights below. I felt mischievous, watching it all from such a powerful height, and thought if I lived here I would sit at the window for hours spying on the tiny, twitching world. I would ride the elevator, too, calling out numbers to the uniformed attendant, who would tip his cap and smile. I would lounge in the lobby or roam the carpeted corridors of the Leamington, trying to guess what was going on behind the countless silent doors.

Miss Higgins did none of these things. She sat and read the *Minneapolis Star* or worked at her embroidery, complaining of a migraine headache. She got them often, she confessed, and could not tolerate much pressure or excitement. I wondered why she chose to stay in such a nervous place.

Supper consisted of cheese and crackers and a can of celery soup, which Miss Higgins heated on her tiny stove. We crowded around her table, feeling almost comfortable.

"It's nice to have visitors," she smiled. "You can call me Anne." We tried but found it difficult to be so casual with Mama's solemn friend.

"I almost married once," Miss Higgins murmured. "I most certainly was asked . . . "

"Did you say no, Miss Higgins?" Peggy asked, astonished. "Didn't you like the fellow well enough?"

Miss Higgins studied the embroidered pansies on her tablecloth. "I liked him quite a lot but it was such a big decision. He wanted me to leave my job and move to Omaha. By the time I thought I might . . . well, he'd found someone else."

"I'm glad that didn't happen to Mama!" Susie exclaimed. "We might never have been born!"

"Or what if she had married someone else—we might be city girls!"

"I think your mom was pretty set on country living. And in all her Minneapolis years she never met a fellow who could match your dad. She'd been sweet on him since high school. I used to steer her down the street so she could read his letters on the way to work."

I pictured Mama weaving down the crowded sidewalk, Miss Higgins guiding her through traffic lights and colorful commotion, and felt immensely satisfied.

Miss Higgins had promised to take us to the WCCO studio to Cedric Adams's Talent Show on our last night in Minneapolis. So many times we had visited that place in our imaginations. Now we would be part of the very same audience we had heard laughing and applauding on the radio.

"I hope everyone's stomach is settled," Miss Higgins worried. "I'm bringing Pepto-Bismol, just in case."

Our stomachs were fine, even after riding two bumping, clanging streetcars to the studio, but Peggy was coming down with a troublesome cold. When we were finally settled in our seats, waiting for Cedric Adams to appear, Peggy blew her nose so hard it gushed with bright red blood. Miss Higgins wanted to stay as badly as we did, but after all her pretty lace hankies were soaked with blood, she guided us outside into a taxi. We were terribly disappointed.

The evening was partially saved when Miss Higgins's neighbor invited us to see her new television set. We huddled around the large walnut Philco, mesmerized by cowboys on horseback galloping across the eight-inch screen.

The next morning we took another cab to a huge, high-ceilinged palace that turned out to be the railroad station. Miss Higgins bought three one-way tickets for Milltown, Wisconsin, and a round-trip ticket for herself. She guided us aboard a coach, and we settled into the plush maroon cushions, Peggy and Miss Higgins facing forward, Susie and I riding backward as the writhing railyard snaked into the distance. We gathered speed and flew past factories and warehouses, clotted city streets and tightly clustered houses, into the peaceful countryside. The barrel-voiced conductor called each stop as we approached: "New Brighton . . . Withrow . . . Maple Island . . . Marine . . . Copas . . . Osceola . . . Dresser Junction . . . " Travelers disembarked at every station; anxious newcomers scanned the coach and settled into place.

"All a-boarrrrrrd!"

Daddy was waiting on the platform of the mustard-colored Milltown depot. We said a hasty good-bye to Miss Higgins, who would take the next train back to Minneapolis, and piled into Daddy's '37 Buick Special, which seemed very cramped and ordinary now.

"Well how about it?" he teased during the short drive home.

"Are you three city slickers ready to give up this fancy life and come home to the farm?"

"Oh Daddy . . . !"

I was ready. Susie and Peggy chattered beside him in the front seat. I sat quietly in back playing with my kaleidoscope, fascinated by its endless bright designs. Each twist revealed a complicated pattern. A gentle shake could recreate the world.

Hotel Leamington
Third Avenue, 10th and 11th Streets
Minneapolis 2, Minnesota
December 21, 1949

Dear Helen,

What I would give for a movie of this past weekend. The girls had fun—but I think I enjoyed it even more.

When we went to bed Saturday night Sara said it seemed like Christmas had come already, but Susan corrected her and said it seemed like the Fair, her birthday, and Christmas all happening at once.

They especially like the hotel elevator, and drove poor Mr. Parkins nearly wild, riding up and down, stopping at every floor.

They have touchy stomachs, I believe, because Susan was car-sick on the trip to Minneapolis and Sara was sick on the Dayton's escalator. Perhaps it was just too much excitement. We attempted to see a broadcast at WCCO on Sunday night, but Peggy's nosebleed spoiled that. We settled instead for a visit with my neighbor, who has just purchased a television set. The little girls were mightily impressed.

They loved the Christmas decorations. We went to

Dayton's which has marvelous animated window displays this year, and a grand Toyland. The dolls didn't hold their attention long, but a woolly black lamb sure did. The escalators, as I said, were very exciting. I lasted with them through Dayton's and part of one dime store. Then either Peggy or Susan spotted a midget eating at the lunch counter and of course were fascinated by her. Sara couldn't see the midget. She wasn't willing to leave without a good look, either. Not being too sharp after such a hectic morning, I thought the midget was a mannikin in a display somewhere and stood in the middle of the floor looking around for her. By that time the girl at the cigar counter was going into hysterics. Finally I realized they must be talking about a human being. Sara kept saying, "Peggy and Susie saw a midget! Can you see a midget*? I don't want to leave until I see the midget!" When they get excited their little voices get louder and louder, and unless the midget was a deaf midget she certainly knew she was the star attraction. Once Sara sighted her, we left in a hurry.*

They are learning to twirl batons, I find. I bought them each an inexpensive baton. By the time I got the three little gals and a roll-away bed and those batons (being twirled) and some balloons into my one room there wasn't much room to spare.

They loved the train ride home, and were awed by a nun in her black and white habit—not to mention the negro porters. By that time they were learning not to point and stare. I don't mind telling you I was exhausted when I finally got back to my apartment Monday evening.

You are doing a fine job, Helen. You can be proud of your girls. Except for nausea and nosebleeds—which they surely couldn't help—they were as good as gold. I wish I could have taken little Teddy, too. That way you might have had a better rest, but a three year old would have been too much for me, I know. I have often fretted about your too-busy life on the farm, with so little culture or convenience. But today I am feeling very alone here, and perhaps a little sorry for myself.

I am knitting a cap and booties for the new baby and will mail it right after the New Year.

Love and Merry Christmas to all—

Anne

Early Losses

In 1949, when I was six years old, I had a reckless love affair with cats. They did not love me in return, for these were farm cats—wild, independent scavengers, too many to know or name. They hunted mice in feed bunks, silo pits, and granaries. They smelled of moldy oats, fermenting silage, fresh manure, and soggy straw.

Daddy fed them generous pans of warm milk from his bucket twice a day at chore time. They came running from all corners—blacks and grays and calicoes—and lapped it eagerly, then scooted into hiding. These cats were quick and scrawny—hard to catch and tough to love. But I was only six, bound to spend myself pursuing the impossible. Susie and Peggy joined in the chase.

We made friends with one big mother cat, calmer and slower than the rest. She allowed us to pet her sleek coat, which was the gray of polished ball bearings. We followed her into the haymow, to the northeast corner where five newborn kittens were sheltered in a nest of broken bales. There we watched them suckle and grow, witnessed the unsealing of their tiny eyes, and brushed their downy fur against our cheeks. We visited too often. Mothercat moved her litter in her mouth, one helpless infant at a time, across a rugged landscape of baled timothy and clover to a deeper, darker hideaway beyond our reach.

The kittens grew up wild, but Mothercat became tame and dependent. We coaxed her into the cellar by leaving plates of table scraps near the trapdoor entrance, then inched her gradually inside. We invited her to play with us in the kitchen when our parents were not around, violating their strict rule: no critters in the house!

The following spring Mothercat bore her babies in a pile of rags we had arranged on the landing of the inside cellar steps. Here we could easily observe the kittens by simply opening the door leading from the kitchen to the damp, dark space below. We could offer milk and table scraps without togging up in bulky clothing, climbing ladders, leaping hay bales, and risking injury in the cliffs and caverns of the mow.

We might have guessed that anything that convenient was a terrible mistake. One early morning my sisters and I opened the cellar door to find Mothercat twirling in anguish. The remains of four dead kittens bloodied the landing and trailed down the cellar steps. Their eyes had been torn out, their entrails ripped from their tiny bellies. Mothercat looked up accusingly and wailed. We ran bare-footed and nightgowned, shrieking, to the barn where our parents were both milking, perched on three-legged stools, their foreheads pressed into their work. They straightened up, startled by our wild entrance.

"The kittens have been murdered!" Peggy cried. "And I'm to blame."

"It's not your fault," said Daddy, stroking her tangled hair. "A tomcat, probably. Must have crept into the cellar through that busted outside door."

"But why?" we cried in unison.

"Some things are hard to understand," said Mama, shaking her

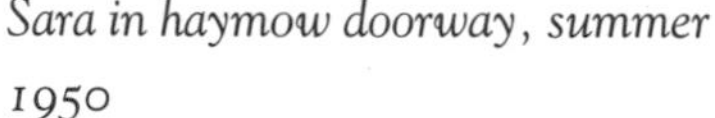

Sara in haymow doorway, summer 1950

Susie, 1950

head. "Now go back to the house, all three of you. Take Mother-cat inside and give her some table scraps. Daddy and I will be there in half an hour."

"I know why this happened," Peggy mourned, as we tiptoed through the dewy grass.

"Because we tamed her?" Susie asked.

"No," sobbed Peggy, inconsolably.

At the age of ten, Peggy felt responsible for everything, including Communism, polio, atomic bombs, and the Korean War. She had tried so hard to pray them all away and failed.

"God must be warning me," she said. "I did not pray enough last night."

In spite of the atrocity, our feline population flourished. By midsummer 1950 we counted thirty cats and almost never saw a rodent. The cats grew skinny and aggressive, stalking the barn walks, crouching underneath the freshened udders, squinting up, eager to catch milk dripping from distended teats. They leaped through bunks and mangers, a gang of clawing, crying savages.

The helpless babies were adorable. We peered into their opaque eyes, studied their featherlight bones, and nosed their fur, perfumed with timothy and fresh alfalfa. We knew the soft, plump kittens would soon be bony beggars, but our love was brave and unconcerned with future grief.

When three bulging mother cats gave birth to large litters in the same week, the haymow was alive with miracles. Susie and I stood reverently on the barn walk below and listened at the open chute. A chorus of mewing echoed from the vaulted timber sky.

One day the loft was silent, and we guessed the cunning mothers had stowed their offspring deeper in the mow. That evening when we went to fetch the cows we heard faint crying in the pasture. We followed the plaintive sound to the edge of the swamp and discovered a gunnysack, soaking wet, cinched tight with baling twine. Susie pulled the sack out of a blackberry thicket and emptied it into the tall, wet grass.

We gasped. Fourteen limp kittens tumbled out, their wet fur plastered tight against their lifeless bodies. Then two began to wriggle and cry as sunlight struck their lidded eyes.

Forgetting the cows completely, we snatched the trembling kittens and ran sobbing to the house.

"Daddy did this, didn't he?"

Mama hesitated a moment. "Yes. The farm will not support so many cats. They'll starve to death—I know you don't want that."

We could not see the logic. We could not forgive so black a deed, nor one so badly bungled. We raged and cried.

"Goddamn Daddy!" Susie gasped.

I was shocked at her language and more amazed to hear myself exclaim, "Damn him to hell!" The only swearing we had ever heard was done by Daddy when he raged against a balky cow or naughty kid or broken-down machine.

Mama's eyes were big and bright behind her thick lenses. She tried to calm us with gentle pats and sympathetic murmurs. When we did not respond to that, she scolded angrily: "Stop it this minute! I have more to worry about than a litter of kittens! I can't have Peggy hearing this—she gets upset so easily. And you might think about your poor, tired father. He'll be in for

Susie (left) and Sara with a couple of cats, 1951

supper soon. Don't let him hear a single nasty word!"

We could not stop. We were hysterical with grief and rage.

"Only a man could do this!" I shouted. "We ought to hunt them all down, tie them up in one big sack, and fling it into the ocean!"

"Yes! Yes!" my twin agreed. "And we would pull them out again and throw the bag into the weeds while some of them were still alive, freezing and choking, dying from pneumonia."

We laughed at our fierce tirade and carried on hilariously until our mother wept. Her tears were thin and silent, but they wrenched the world apart.

"We didn't mean it, Mama."

"We wouldn't drown the men—especially not Daddy. We'll be quiet, we won't say another hateful thing."

Mama found an eye dropper in the medicine cabinet and suggested that we try to nurse the kittens back to health.

Despite our patient efforts, the fragile gray kitten perished in a day. We named the calico Survivor. She grew strong and raised a dozen healthy litters.

"Cats are fine, within reason, of course," Daddy observed a few weeks later when he felt forgiveness was at hand. "But what we really need now is a dog—a collie bred to work with sheep and cattle."

He brought that collie home one day, a sharp-eyed puppy in a cardboard box: Jeanie, of Balsam Acres. She was a purebred collie, golden brown with snowy feet and collar, like the one Daddy said he had owned when he was a boy.

He admitted to Mama that he had paid a fancy price.

"A fool thing, probably—a mutt would do as well." We knew he did not mean it. He sounded proud of his extravagance, his willingness to pay for beauty and breeding.

Jeanie grew up brave and loyal, willing to work at corralling the cows, nipping their hocks, rounding up the strays and laggards. She was equally ready for play. We romped and rolled with her in the soft summer grass, buried our faces in her coat, and adorned her neck with leis of dandelions and clover.

The following summer Jeanie discovered that if kids and cows were good for chasing, cars were faster and better. At first she sprinted in the shallow ditches of County Road I, then raced along the shoulder. All through August Jeanie ran the blacktop, testing her endurance neck and neck with cars and pickups, barking sharply at their whirling tires.

She ignored all reprimands. Daddy did not want to tie her, insisting that a collie on a leash was worse than no dog at all.

Finally she tangled with the bumper of a passing truck that tore the skin from her throat and laid her chest bloody and bare. Daddy carried Jeanie from the weedy ditch and placed her in the shade of a massive oak behind the house.

"Poor fool dog," he murmured. "Poor fool dog."

Jeanie's eyes were glazed, and a low growl rumbled from her torn throat.

"You kids get in the house!"

Minutes later we heard the crack of his rifle. We looked out the kitchen window and saw Daddy sitting near the collie.

That evening he asked us to select a burial site for Jeanie. We chose the western border of our backyard near a wooded slope we called the Violet Hill for its profusion of blue and yellow violets every spring. It had been one of Jeanie's favorite runs.

Daddy shoveled out a deep, wide vault and laid the collie down inside. "Is that okay with you?" he asked as he surveyed the mourners.

"Just fine."

"Can we arrange her legs to look like she's racing down the hill?" asked Susie.

"Good idea."

Daddy waited patiently while we positioned Jeanie for a joyful chase. When we were satisfied, he sprinkled lime across her body. We did not need to ask the reason, for we had seen him lime the shallow graves of cows and sheep to hasten their decay. We knelt together by the grave and with our forearms rolled the dark earth down until our collie's golden coat had vanished like a setting sun.

Jeanie's funeral was the first of many. The burial ground became a sacred place, visited in times of peace as well as pain. We had chosen the site carefully, under a canopy of oaks where the clipped grass met the wild woodlands. Round, white stones collected from the pasture formed its borders. My sisters and I chopped and carved and spaded up the tangled mat of weeds within. We sifted and raked the loamy soil with bare hands, relishing the cool, damp dirt that stained our knuckles and lodged beneath our fingernails.

The headstones were boulders unearthed by the plow. There was a fresh, abundant crop of rocks each spring after the winter frost had heaved them to the surface. Daddy encouraged us to help ourselves—take them all, for heaven's sake. We were choosy, selecting oval monuments with flat, smooth faces. We scrubbed them clean with Oxydol and crayoned our inscriptions:

> Here Lies Jeanie, Faithful Collie, Buried 8/16/50
> Limey, the Lorikeet, Killed by a Cat, 9/3/50

And alongside:

> Felix the Cat; Repent and Know Thy God

We did not mind that our epitaphs would wear away in one or two brief seasons. We would not forget a single rabbit, cat, or turtle or where we had laid them out to rest.

Peggy presided at the funerals. She dressed up in a long black cape smuggled from the back of Mama's closet. Peggy liked to read long and loud from the Holy Scriptures, insisting that Susie and I sing and pray in the background.

> Rock of ages, cleft for me,
> Let me hide myself in Thee . . .

Susie and I liked the game better when our cousin, Leanne, joined in. Like us, she had just turned seven. Nearly all of our cousins were loud, silly boys, and we were delighted to have Leanne as a playmate. She lived six miles away on a farm near Milltown, but Mama's brother, Uncle Leland, drove her all the way to our house for many fun-filled summer visits. Sometimes she stayed for several days, and occasionally Daddy took us to spend an afternoon with her. Leanne was an only daughter with a wealth of toys to share. Susie and I admitted privately to feeling jealous of her books and dolls and store-bought dresses. On the other hand, she had to wear thick glasses, and she wet her pants a lot, which meant she was teased terribly at school. Somehow our cousin's handicaps helped to steady the friendship.

Leanne enjoyed the funerals, and she was bursting with creative ideas.

"How would *you* like to be wrapped in nothing but an old rag?" she asked indignantly. "The coffin is important. It should be lined with silk or something. And there ought to be some flowers."

We swiped slices of satiny fabric from Mama's sewing basket to use as lining for the shoe boxes. We scattered wild rose petals as we sang the hymns and beautified the graveyard with wild sweet pea and columbine.

It was a wet summer, and the earth was rich with angleworms.

Leanne suggested we should be using airtight coffins. We began keeping a supply of mason jars stashed under the back porch, and we looked for dead birds and other small cadavers that fit comfortably inside.

Peggy refused to sermonize at such funerals. It did not mean a thing, she said, unless there was real grief involved. So she made us plant our "experiments" in a separate, newly opened section roped off from the sacred burial ground. No fair burying anything that was already half decayed. We must not use stone markers, either; only temporary crosses made from lath and loops of baling twine should mark these lesser graves.

We agreed to Peggy's conditions. They were reasonable enough. Besides, this was our chance to wear the robes and invent our own rituals without a bossy older sister hanging around to ridicule our efforts.

One afternoon Leanne, Susie, and I decided to sneak out to the cemetery and unearth a glass container to see how the dearly departed was faring. We were shocked to discover that worms had somehow entered the burial chamber and were feeding on the rotting carcass.

Maybe it would take more practice. We didn't pray as long or well as Peggy, and we could have forgotten to tighten down the lid.

Leanne turned her face away and gave the lid an extra twist. We quickly buried it again, piling the dirt extra high, patting the mound until it appeared perfect, undisturbed. We didn't check a second time.

On an April day in 1951, eight-year-old Leanne was buried in the damp, spring earth. I did not actually see her coffin settled in the ground; Mama and Daddy brought us all straight home after the funeral service. But I recall the smell of lemon polish and the freshly starched lace curtains veiling narrow windows in a farmhouse parlor. I remember rosy, floral rugs covered by rows of slatted wooden chairs borrowed from the church basement. The mourners sat stiffly in their seats, yet the chairs squeaked and rattled through the sermon, as if protesting every word.

Pastor Hendrickson praised God for guiding His little lamb through earthly storms and deep, dark valleys. He praised the Lord for calling her home to heavenly pastures where she would dwell with Him forever. His praises finally completed, the pastor asked everyone to join him in the Lord's Prayer. I felt confused and angry and not at all like praying.

A sharp, vibrato voice began singing Leanne's favorite hymn from Sunday school: "Jesus loves me, this I know . . . "

My twin burst into startled laughter. The chairs rattled as everyone turned to find out who had lost control.

> . . . For the Bible tells me so.
> Little ones to Him belong,
> They are weak but He is strong.
> Yes, Jesus loves me, yes, Jesus loves me,
> Yes, Jesus loves me, the Bible tells me so.

Mama led us into the adjacent bedroom where our cousin lay in her satin-lined casket. Vases of fragrant pink roses stood on either side. Leanne was beautiful. She wore her Sunday best, a deep blue taffeta dress with a lace-trimmed yoke. The shiny fabric reflected different colors, like a rainbow in the sun-washed sky. Now it would be buried in the ground. Leanne's eyes were closed and her glasses gone. Her silky hair was arranged in perfect spring curls, crowned by a huge white bow.

"You can touch her," Mama urged. "This is our time to say good-bye."

"Yes, better touch her now," said Grandma Williamson. "It's the last chance you're ever going to get." I looked up at Grandma's wobbling chin and knew she had not meant to sound so angry.

I pressed my finger to Leanne's forehead. She was hard as a rubber doll. "How can she be dead, Mama? Just last week we played on the swings! The next day she got sick—but Aunty Violet said it was only measles."

"It started out that way—she was getting better for awhile, then she got very sick with brain fever. The doctor called it encephalitis."

Two men in dark gray suits wheeled Leanne's coffin out of the bedroom, through the cramped kitchen, and onto the back porch, past her roller skates, her bicycle. Her airplane swing, gliding empty in the wind.

Aunty Violet was there suddenly with arms and legs outstretched, blocking the way. A low moan sounded in her throat. The men carried her, kicking and thrashing, to the funeral car. *No, no, you can't take my Leanne!* Uncle Leland climbed in behind and closed the door.

We did not follow the string of cars heading north on Highway 35 toward the Milltown cemetery but turned east instead onto a gravel road that took us home. Daddy said it had been a long, exhausting day. It was time to feed the livestock. The kids looked tired and hungry, too.

At the supper table Mama and Daddy carried on the usual talk—which heifers were freshening, which fields were dry enough to plow. They would plant corn on the east twenty this year; the north field was too depleted—better seed it with alfalfa.

Susie and I didn't talk about our cousin either. I didn't want to ask her if she felt like me—more curious than bereaved, as if I were standing back, observing a wicked experiment with death. I remembered Peggy's words: Unless there is real grief involved, it doesn't mean a thing.

I couldn't make the feelings come; it seemed that Susie couldn't either. Instead we planned to do the dishes every day without complaining. We would cut the grass ourselves this year and help Mama weed the garden. Another thing: we wouldn't do those funerals anymore. We were too old for such a childish game.

That summer a couple of cats got into some rat poison, and we asked Daddy to bury them in the pasture. Our graveyard was forgotten. The wooden crosses soon collapsed. The headstones vanished in a tangle of pasture rose and meadowsweet.

Priscilla

By the time Priscilla was born in 1950, large families were going out of style. Three or four children was the rule in town, at least for Protestants. Five or more meant you were Roman Catholic, raising babies for the Pope. Prolific farmers might be denounced as ignorant or greedy—intentionally producing their own crew of unpaid harvest hands.

A self-conscious fourth grader, Peggy felt embarrassed that Mama was expecting another baby, and she warned my twin and me not to broadcast it at school.

"Why not?" we asked in unison.

"Five kids are just too many. The kids will call us stupid *farmers*."

"We *are* farmers!"

"Besides, when Teddy was born my first-grade teacher made the whole class sing 'Rock-A-Bye-Baby.' "

"That doesn't seem so bad."

"Well, then, I'll tell you something *really* awful—Alex Anderson says a baby proves your parents *do it*."

She whispered those last words with tears collecting in her violet eyes. My twin and I had no idea what shameful thing our parents could be doing. They were too tired after evening chores to visit dance halls or taverns, like some of their less ambitious neighbors. They kept no alcohol at home. Mama even disapproved of coffee, insisting that it set a person's nerves on edge.

My twin and I felt mystified, yet didn't question Peggy further. We had seen the bullies chase and tease her—"Piggy! Piggy! Oink—oink—*oink!*"—and we didn't want to cause her more grief. We vowed not to talk about the baby with our teachers or classmates or anyone outside the family.

We had all felt anxious about Mama's pregnancy for several weeks, ever since our parents' bedtime conversation had sifted through the open grate in our bedroom floor. Mama had sounded so discouraged. Daddy had tried hard to cheer her up:

"I feel so old and tired—I just don't have the energy for this."

"At thirty-five? Oh, Helen. I've let you work too hard. I'll find a hired man or else reduce the herd."

"We can't afford that, Harvey. Besides, it's not the farm work that exhausts me. Cows are easy, compared with kids. I just can't think of managing all those bottles and diapers again. Why did this have to happen now, when Teddy is finally toilet trained and Peggy's old enough to babysit?"

"Things will work out fine in the long run," Daddy promised. "I'm betting on a boy. That would be fine, wouldn't it? A partner for Teddy? Hell, maybe they'll incorporate someday. Hellerud Brothers' Registered Holsteins. A first-class operation." They named the unborn baby Thomas. "Teddy and Tommy," Mama called her boys, sounding pleased as the event drew near.

They got another girl and had to scramble for a name. Their hasty choice—Priscilla—sounded like a frilly, ruffled curtain. It didn't suit this sturdy kid at all.

"Congratulations on your baby sister!" Miss Paulson exclaimed before the entire combined first- and second-grade class.

"What sister?" we replied with vacant eyes.

"Priscilla Elaine Hellerud, eight pounds, three ounces!" Miss

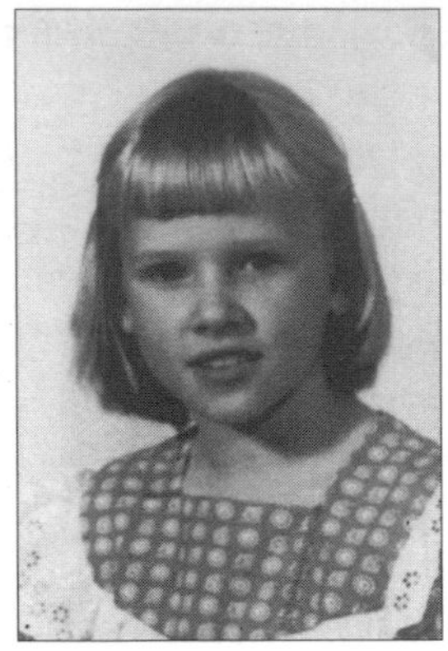

Susie (left) and Sara in second-grade photos

Paulson persisted. "I read her birth announcement in the *Polk County Ledger*."

"Oh, yeah . . . "

"She's such a good baby—so quiet, we just forgot about her."

That part was nearly true. The baby was a sleeper who seldom fussed or cried. She had a full, bold-featured Hellerud face, so different from her dainty, heart-faced siblings. And she held her rattle with a firm, left-handed grip. Daddy said Priscilla was a southpaw, just like him. He adored her.

By the time Priscilla was one year old, Mama was doing heavy duty in the barn. "Midwinter is our toughest time," she said, "with pens and gutters to be cleaned, frozen pipes and water cups to thaw, silage to chip and haul. Daddy can't do all this alone. I know I can count on you big girls to clean up the dishes and watch Teddy and Priscilla."

This might have been acceptable if Susie and Peggy had done their share. Peggy washed the dishes quickly and piled them on the drainboard, then fled to her bedroom with her fifth-grade homework and her straight A expectations. Susie, who had been taking piano lessons for about six months, practiced every night with almost frightening concentration. I was stuck with entertaining two rambunctious kids. Sometimes I abandoned them and entertained myself, escaping to the upstairs storeroom. There I could drape myself in discarded curtains and writhe like Salome or climb into Mama's cast-off city suits and hats and platform pumps, emerging as a private secretary.

My favorite flight took me to an ancient land I knew from Sunday school. The Book of Esther thrilled me. I saw the palace courtyard, with its "green and blue hangings fastened with cords of fine linen and purple to silver rings and pillars of marble," exactly as the Bible described it. I memorized some crucial passages:

> And the maiden Esther pleased the King . . . and he speedily gave her things for purification . . . Now every maid's turn was come to go in to the King Ahasuerus, after she had been twelve months, according to the manner of the women, six months with oil of myrrh and six months with sweet odors . . .
>
> So Esther was taken unto King Ahasuerus into his house royal. And the King loved Esther above all the women and she obtained grace and favor in his sight more than all the virgins; so that he set the royal crown upon her head and made her Queen.

I had been favored over all the rest. I crowned myself with an inverted lampshade and wrapped my body in a bolt of lining fabric, blue as the summer sky. There, reflected in the dense Wisconsin night that silvered the storeroom window like a looking glass, stood Esther, Queen of Persia.

One winter evening in 1951, I heard King Ahasuerus summoning his Queen. I had to go. I set Teddy on the kitchen floor with a box of Tinker Toys. Using a dish towel, I tied Priscilla into the ladderback rocker in her favorite position—standing backward, pumping vigorously—then slipped the centuries.

I was swathed in royal raiment, prepared to meet my king, when Priscilla's screaming pierced my fantasy. I fled the palace, still wound in fabric attached to the cardboard bolt. It lodged in the stairwell and spewed a rayon river down the stairs, through the hallway, into the parlor where I found Priscilla on her back beneath the capsized rocker, blood flowing from her mouth. Peggy and Susie crouched beside her.

Peggy looked up frantically as I approached.

"Where have you been? I thought you were watching her!"

"I *was!*"

"Then why are you wrapped like a mummy? Here—help me lift this chair."

Together we hoisted the rocker, and Priscilla came up like a whipped sailor bound to the mast. When she opened her mouth to scream again I saw a strip of flesh dangling long and loose as an angleworm.

"Oh God," I gasped, "she's bitten off her tongue!"

"Go to the barn and get Mama—no, you can't, all tangled up like that. I'll go! Just rock her—and pray! Susie, play a lullaby or something."

Susie grabbed the Lutheran songbook and raced through a couple of hymns. I can't remember what she played. Maybe "O, Sacred Head Now Wounded" or "O, For a Thousand Tongues."

Mama rushed into the room, not even stopping to remove her barn boots. She said the wound was serious and sent Daddy to the neighbors where he telephoned for Dr. Hoff. The doctor came within the hour. He thought Priscilla's tongue could be repaired, but he would have to take her to Amery Hospital for anesthesia. Mama bundled up the howling child, and they sped away. Dr. Hoff returned our exhausted mother and pale, sleepy sister the following afternoon.

Priscilla mended without lasting scars, except for a lisping patchwork tongue and a firm refusal to eat red foods, which—

right or wrong—I always blamed on the bloody accident.

I waited for some healing punishment, which neither Mama nor Daddy delivered.

"I'll have to rearrange my work somehow," Mama said. "I've been expecting way too much of you." Later she added: "Take that flimsy yardage that you like so well. I bought it at the Ben Franklin fire sale for next to nothing . . . cut it up and make a gown if you want to."

I didn't feel like the Queen of Persia anymore. Permission seemed to hold me back somehow. And I was soaked with guilt, like the stain on the braided rug where Prissy fell—a splotch of deep maroon that marked the tightly cabled wool clear through.

Close Calculations

Once a year, late in January, Mama claimed the dining room as her accounting office for two or three full days. She spilled the contents of several large manila envelopes onto the round oak table, then sorted check stubs, statements, and receipts into tidy rubber-banded stacks. That done, she worked long columns of arithmetic, entered totals in her ledgers, calculated profits, losses, and depreciation, prepared the tax return, and planned a budget for the coming year.

Mama recorded actual income and expenses to the penny, as she had been trained to do at Minneapolis Business College. The budget was expressed in rounded figures with a little slack built in for mediocre crops, sick cattle, or machinery repairs. She never planned on big disasters. As Mama said, a farmer's days turned on hard work and discipline; the long-term outlook hinged on luck and faith.

In 1951 Mama projected total farm income at thirty-six hundred dollars, or three hundred dollars per month. Farm expenses, mortgage payments, and taxes would eat up two-thirds of that. She figured she could run the household for twelve months on an even thousand dollars, including one hundred dollars for Faith Lutheran Church and thirty for a generous Christmas. That left a two-hundred-dollar surplus for unexpected costs or possibly some contribution to a savings plan.

When Mama's debits, credits, gains, or losses had been balanced and her budget drafted, she conferred with Daddy who would nod agreeably at her reports. Sometimes he offered mild comments or suggestions.

"Look at that—$190 for the vet last year! That's more than all our doctor bills combined, including Prissy's birth."

"The vet was reasonable enough, considering we had two major hardware cases, and a twisted gut. We *have* been lucky with the kids, discounting Susie's broken leg in 1949."

"Well, costs are rising. Do you think we ought to buy that Blue Cross plan through the Farm Bureau?"

Mama shook her head. "I don't like betting against myself that way. I still say a healthy attitude is the best medical insurance. A person is as fit as he expects to be—barring accidents, of course. And I prefer to think we won't have any more of those."

It was two weeks later—mid-February 1951—that Priscilla nearly bit her tongue off when she capsized with the rocker. Tongue-patching was not in the budget; a yearling ewe was sold to satisfy the bill. That spring, after weeks of throat infections, Susie, Peggy, and I had our tonsils taken out, costing a heifer calf apiece.

The summer was unusually hot and dry, without sufficient moisture for a healthy stand of corn or oats. Milk production faltered during August due to thinning pasture and oppressive heat.

Mama's midyear calculations showed the dairy operation running into serious losses.

"Look at those sluggish cattle—I'm beginning to suspect acetonemia," Mama fretted. She consulted with the vet, who concurred with Mama's diagnosis, recommending daily doses of Herd Tonic and molasses for the Holsteins.

"You need a tonic, too," said Daddy, pointing out her pallor, sunken eyes, and listless appetite. "I think you ought to see the doctor, Helen."

"It's just a touchy stomach. I know what to do for that." Mama went on a milk-toast and soda-cracker diet. At chore time she drank dippers of soothing milk straight from the cans before we pounded down the lids.

"Please, Helen! If you won't see the doctor, at least get yourself to bed. You call the vet at the first sign of trouble, but you refuse to take care of yourself."

"It's nothing but the flu. It just has to run its course," Mama assured him. "I might as well make myself useful in the meantime, instead of dwelling on the way I feel."

A few days later Mama fainted at the supper table. She clutched the tabletop for balance, then slid sideways to the floor, taking a Jell-O salad and a bowl of mashed potatoes with her.

Daddy leaped out of his chair. "I'm driving Mama to that new hospital in Centuria. It's only five miles away." His voice quavered. "Now be good kids—Peggy, you're in charge. I'll be back just as soon as I can."

We learned later that we had nearly lost our mother. She had been suffering from bleeding ulcers—undetected, since use of the outdoor toilet prevented her from noticing her bloody stool. She had convinced herself that it was only a persistent diarrhea.

"Doctor said she was running on only half a tank," Daddy reported, still shaken by the thought of his near loss. "Good thing she didn't faint out in the woods today when she was picking berries—she might have lain there for hours."

Mama stayed in the hospital several days and nights, receiving medications and transfusions and a badly needed rest.

Daddy gave eight pints of blood that year, being obligated to replenish the supply. He would make additional donations to the blood bank every year thereafter, all his life, small payments on a moral debt too large to satisfy.

I did not hear my parents' fiscal conference in January 1952, but I can recreate a likely scene.

Mama would have made some rueful mention of the remaining bills and shaken her head over the disappointing deficit.

"That ulcer was a costly business. If I hadn't been so stubborn..."

I imagine Daddy teased her just a little. "What? No money set aside next year for hospitals? I guess you think that brand-new blood supply came with some kind of guarantee."

Or he may have offered some consoling words. "Ben Franklin would agree with your philosophy. He said 'Nothing is more fatal to health than the overcare of it.'"

Mama would have countered with another Franklin observation: "'God cures; the doctor takes the fees.'"

Dynamite

Peggy, Susie, and I played often at the kitchen table, clipping costumes to the waists and shoulders of our paper dolls. Mama swept and scrubbed around us, glad to see us playing so contentedly on dismal days. But this was more than rainy day amusement: this was a magic flight on paper wings. Peggy became Sonja Henie, the figure-skating queen. Susie was a New York City ballerina named Holly Ann Bergman. I called myself Rochelle, Mistress of the Flying Trapeze.

The doll books came with all the latest fashions—cashmere sweaters flung across the shoulders, held in place by golden chains; billowing circle skirts; long, skinny sheaths; strapless formals; shorty coats, unbuttoned, flaring in the breeze.

Our glamorous performers needed more: leotards and tutus, spangled costumes, capes and crowns. We created these ourselves from wrapping paper, paint and crayons, glue and glitter, bright buttons and silver stars.

Little Priscilla, only a toddler, was barred from the game. Six-year-old Teddy watched with interest. "Can I play too?" he asked one rainy afternoon.

"This is girl stuff," Peggy said. "Boys aren't supposed to play with dolls."

"Who says?"

"Suppose we let you play with us. Who are you going to be?"

"Sears Roebuck?" Teddy suggested timidly, grasping for a firm identity.

"Ha!" our older sister hooted. "He wants to be a catalog!"

Susie's face brightened. "Wait—that gives me a great idea! Think of all the great clothes we could copy from the catalog. We could even cut out models and make ourselves some brand new dolls."

We raced for the Sears Roebuck and Montgomery Ward catalogs, ignoring our bewildered brother in a surge of creativity.

Sometime that evening Holly Ann Bergman's dancing legs were ripped from her body. Rochelle became a Headless Wonder. Sonja Henie simply vanished from the rink.

We sought revenge. Tormenting Teddy was no problem. He had a dynamite temper, and we knew exactly how to light his fuse. Peggy called him "Teddy-Girl," pointing out his dimples, long lashes, wavy hair, and small size. She was incensed that the only boy had been rewarded with those pretty features and felt compelled to make him pay. Susie and I named our little brother "Banty," comparing him to Mama's bantam roosters, or "Shrimp Bones," which made him spin with rage. Susie played his theme song—"Shrimp Boats Are A-Comin' "—on the piano whenever he passed by the parlor. Teddy flailed like a windmill with a broken rudder, and he pummeled her until the music stopped.

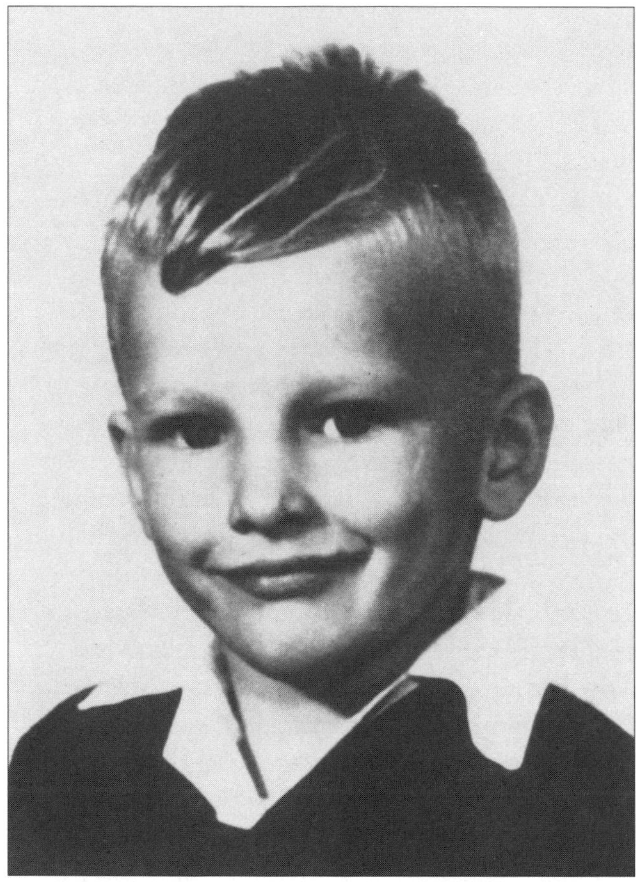

Teddy, age seven

We usually saved such mean-spirited teasing for occasions when our parents weren't around. Yet Daddy must have sensed a problem. "I think we need to get you away from all these girls," he winked at Teddy across the supper table. "How about you and me going up on the Breakin' tomorrow to blast some stumps . . . "

"Harvey!" Mama interrupted. "That's no job for a six-year-old. It's dangerous enough for you, without a kid to mind."

Teddy's eyes grew bright. "Why do you call it the Breakin', Daddy?"

"Because it's wild land I'm breaking. I've cut the trees, and now I'm dynamiting stumps, breaking it for pasture. For the sheep."

"Can I go with? Can I, Mama?"

"Well, I suppose, if one of your older sisters goes along."

Peggy had a stack of ironing to tackle, and Susie planned to practice the piano, so I was elected to be Teddy's chaperon.

The next morning Daddy led us a quarter mile through the rolling pasture, up to the Breakin', and we blasted stumps. I had explored this place when it was still a leafy hardwood forest; now it was a shocking wasteland full of shattered stumps and craters, dust and dirt, and miniature mountains teeming with vicious red ants. Daddy said the Breakin' would become a pasture for the sheep; yet I could not imagine his flock of Hampshires grazing in these ruins.

Daddy gave us no time to wonder at it. He had serious work to do, and he was counting on his son's assistance.

I watched from a cautious distance while they tackled two small stumps. One got a charge of two sticks, the other three. After a thunderous explosion there was nothing left except two ugly pockmarks in the earth. Next they attacked a larger stump with five sticks, lit the fuses, and ran for shelter behind a nearby oak. *Boom!* Only a few torn roots remained. Daddy instructed Teddy to plant three more sticks of dynamite that would eradicate the shards. They lit three fuses, but there were only two loud booms, two fountains of debris. One stick had failed to detonate.

"Don't look," warned Daddy, as he crept close to make a brave investigation.

I peeked. I watched him poking in the wreckage, leaping backward just in time to dodge the explosion. I watched and wondered at my father, who loved the birds and trees and wild flowers, yet seemed to relish this amazing demolition.

"Stay back, Ted! I'm going to do a dance!" laughed Daddy as he doled out eight sticks of dynamite to eight small stumps, then lit the fuses one by one. *Pop-pop-pop-pop-pop-pop-pop-pop!*

He leapt from blast to blast, as agile as an acrobat. My brother squealed with glee.

Another challenge followed—a huge oak stump with a nearly perfect root structure. Daddy used a stout stick to probe it all around but could not find sufficient space to make a tunnel for the charge. After more puzzling and poking, he finally found a small opening and scooped it out with his gloved hands.

"Come 'ere, Ted," he called. "We want to do this right the first time, so we're going to light ten sticks."

They ignited all ten fuses, and we started home for supper. We were walking backward as she blew. The dirt was visible before the sound was heard. Impressive. When we returned the next day, only a deep crater marked the place where the toughest stump once stood. The following week Daddy discovered a small piece in the west hayfield.

"My Gawd, Teddy, look at that! We gave that stump a quarter mile ride!" That was the only fragment ever found.

A week later Daddy returned his leftover dynamite to Dahlstrom's hardware store in Balsam Lake. Teddy was upset that Daddy was not keeping it. He rode in the back seat of the Buick with the dynamite on its return journey. Years later he confessed to placing two sticks and a length of fuse under the front seat so he could keep them for emergencies. When he got home he hid his weapons in a cubby under the cellar steps.

Daddy had explained that dynamite was not dangerous by itself; it would not explode without a detonator. That hardly mattered. His sisters didn't understand a thing about it. He could chase them with his blazing explosives and see them truly terrified. Once or twice he burned his fingers as he practiced lighting up the fuse, but it was worth the trouble. Now he could tolerate the teasing. He even welcomed it. The stash of dynamite made him feel powerful. Prepared for anything.

The Pickle Patch

In the early 1950s, with five growing children and mounting household expenses, Mama decided that growing cucumbers might be a way to raise some extra cash. So we grew "cukes," countless bushels of them, four summers running.

Mama first got the notion from a neighbor, Jug Johnson, who ran a marginal dairy operation just across the road. Jug dried his cows up every summer—just as the pasturelands grew lush and milk production should have peaked—so he could hire out to Gedney's pickle salting station in Centuria. I could tell from Mama's tone of voice that she did not approve of such haphazard dairy farming. Still, Jug said that Gedney paid him good money, more than his skimpy checks from the Land O' Lakes creamery had ever been. The growers were well compensated, too.

Well, Mama planned to find that out, first hand. And she wouldn't compromise the milking either.

Daddy said, "Try it and see."

An abandoned barnyard—about one-third of an acre behind an old barn, caved and silver with age—provided fertile soil for the pickle patch. In mid-May Daddy plowed and disked and raked the ground. Mama drove to the Gedney station and signed on as a grower. She brought back a sack of flat, white seeds and promised us gainful employment as soon as school was out.

Our first assignment was to follow Mama and her hoe, dropping ten or twelve seeds at a time into the carefully made beds. We then covered them with dirt, mounding it up into tidy hills ringed by little ditches for efficient irrigation. We chattered happily about the shopping spree we would enjoy before school started in the fall.

"I'm going to buy new saddle shoes!" Peggy exclaimed. "And nylon underpants—in seven different colors—one for every day of the week!"

Susie and I planned to purchase matching red sweaters, finger mits to replace our bulky home-knit mittens, and headbands to control our wispy hair.

Mama warned us not to "count the chickens before they hatched." There was hard work ahead—as well as the element of weather, which could wither or drown our profits. But if we stuck faithfully to the task, we could expect some measure of reward.

After the late May planting, we watched and waited for the fuzzy three-pronged plants, which finally emerged with split seed casings stuck to the tips of the leaves. Soon it would be time to thin the hills, leaving four strong survivors. During a later thinning we would reduce the plants to two, then train them to crawl in opposite directions. Mama showed us how to direct the vines into rows for easier picking. Susie could not see why this was necessary and argued that each plant should be allowed to roam wherever it pleased.

"If they aren't laid out neatly, you won't be able to walk without smashing your crop," Mama insisted.

We continued to help with weeding and watering. The patch flourished. As the weather grew hotter, we allowed ourselves short breaks, which included running down the hill and jumping into the creek that flowed beyond the tumbling barn. Mama did not have time for such recreation. Her midday "break" was usually spent in the kitchen, making dinner for her hungry crew. We often found that she had straightened and untangled vines and weeded a row or two early in the morning before the sun got hot, before we kids were even out of bed.

By late July we could hardly wait to pick the first pickle. Mama assigned four long rows to each of us and issued individual burlap sacks tagged with our names. We had to pick our designated rows at least twice a week and every second day during the height of the season. Our backs ached. Our arms and hands were scratched and itchy from the vines and the annoying little stickers that defended every piece of fruit.

Teddy was too young for serious picking, but he liked to hang around the pickle patch and lend a hand to any sister who had been kind or clever enough to pay him special attention. Priscilla, who was only a toddler, was no help at all. She liked to collect the pretty yellow blossoms and stuff them in her pockets. She wandered through the rows, jabbering to the plants. When Mama scolded Priscilla for picking wee nubbins, she defended herself: "I asked this little cute-nunner if he was ready, and he didn't say a thing, so I picked him anyway!"

After that we had to take turns babysitting to keep our little sister well away from the patch.

While it was possible to pick the cukes too small, we were also careful not to let them grow too large. The dainty ones—about two and a half inches long—were used for sweet gherkins and would grade as number ones. The factory paid the most for this size. The next size—about three to six inches—became dill pickles and brought only half as much. I'm not sure what was done with the number threes, but Mama told us we were losing money if we let any of our cucumbers get that big. Finding a "jumbo" in your row, which was barely worth its trip to the factory, meant that you had really been sloppy. These huge ones sapped energy from the vines—energy that should have gone into producing the profitable number ones, according to our mother.

Day by day we filled our sacks and learned that thorough work paid off because, as Mama said, "If you have to pick them anyway, you might as well get the top price."

Twice a week we all looked forward to dragging our sacks of cucumbers from the dark tool shed that kept them cool, loading them into the trunk of the Buick, and driving to the old wooden Gedney station in Centuria, five winding miles to the west.

Mama, Peggy, Susie, and I had our cucumbers graded separately. Three silent, kerchiefed women sorted the cucumbers into wooden boxes as our crop rode past on a wide conveyer belt. Susie and I thought one of the women graded our pickings too strictly. She threw many cucumbers into the number two box, small ones that we thought were rightfully number ones. We discussed this with Mama, and she fully agreed. There was nothing to be done, however, except to hope the next time we brought our cukes into the factory, this woman might be absent. But she was a faithful worker, nearly always on the job.

Frequently, after watching the grading, my sisters and I wandered into the back area of the station where huge, deep, round vats held pickles in various stages of the curing process. What would happen, I wondered, if some kid fell into one of those vats? Would he sink or swim? How would the two men who worked there manage to fish him out? How quickly would a kid be pickled in that strong-smelling brine?

After collecting our grading slips from Jug Johnson, who managed the scales, we presented them at the payout window and received our cash. Our individual earnings were usually about a dollar—close to two for a hefty three-day August picking. Mama guarded our monies, placing them carefully into four separate envelopes inside her purse.

The next stop was Peterson's Grocery. During the summer months we ate a lot of vegetables from the garden, and Mama bought only her staples—tea, sugar, salt, flour, maybe some spices. We might just as well wait in the car, minding Teddy and Priscilla, Mama said, rather than trooping through the crowded aisles. She reminded us that cucumber money must be saved for clothes and school supplies, never squandered on candy or temptations such as paper dolls or comic books.

Usually our earnings from the cucumber patch totaled about a hundred dollars, including Mama's pickings. Our best summer—1953—we made nearly $120. Most of our profits went for shoes, socks, underwear, and sweaters for the coming year. We were each allowed to choose our own pencils, writing tablets, erasers, and crayons—and pay for them as well. After a sweaty summer of planting, thinning, training, weeding, watering, and picking, our shopping trip to Ben Franklin for school supplies was a grand reward. Now we felt ready for study, eager to tackle the next grade.

The pickle patch had been our summer school. Mama pointed out one of its lessons in her plain-spoken way: "When you've had to stand on your head for hours picking cukes in the hot sun, you won't be inclined to spend your earnings foolishly."

Dear Aunt Polly

I have always been impressed by rural mailboxes—those domed receptacles that, since the advent of Rural Free Delivery in the 1930s, bring the wider world to isolated country lanes in spite of rain or hail or sleet or snow, six days out of seven. They can accommodate small packages, a party invitation, international news, and sweepstakes promises, all in one fruitful delivery.

During the early 1950s our address was simply Star Route,

Balsam Lake, Wisconsin. Our world was not so vast nor so complex that it required Zip Codes. We had a standard mailbox of bright aluminum wide and high enough to hold a pair of shoes from Sears Roebuck, long enough to house the *St. Paul Sunday Pioneer Press*. Mounted on a four-by-four and planted in a milk can filled with sand and gravel, our mailbox stood in a patch of purple clover where our long sloping driveway entered County Road I. We furnished the interior with a mason jar lid to hold coins for postage due or for the three-cent stamp we might not have on hand. Daddy painted his name across the left side in bold black letters: H H Hellerud. The right side was fitted with a red metal flag to signal the mailman when we had mail for pickup, in case he had none to deliver and planned to speed on by.

That seldom was the case. The mailman delivered something nearly every day—a seed catalog, the Royal Neighbors' circular, the bill from Polk-Burnett Electric, now and then a first-class letter. Mail time was 1:15 P.M. Daddy timed his dinner carefully so he could fetch the mail, as if he were waiting for a secret windfall. He stood behind the lilacs when the mail car approached, as if sheltering his hopes and expectations. Once the car disappeared around the bend, he set off with long strides to collect and examine his reward. He usually trudged back up the hill and tossed the disappointing mail on the kitchen table. Maybe tomorrow. Tomorrow was another day, another delivery.

"What is Daddy expecting in the mail?" I asked Mama, guessing her answer in advance.

"I don't know, Sara—I expect he doesn't either. Some folks need surprises, and farmers get precious few of those, unless you want to count the weather."

It was clear that mail time meant promises and possibilities. Peggy, Susie, and I began racing Daddy to the box. Seldom was there any mail for us, so we decided to improve our luck. We clipped mail-in coupons from the magazines, printed our names and addresses neatly on the dotted lines, and glued them to penny postcards. We propped them up inside the box, raised the flag, and waited. Soon we began receiving colorful travel brochures, booklets on baby care and household hints, free samples of feminine hygiene products—complete with diagramed instructions for their use. Mama confiscated our trial box of Tampax before we even got to open it. "You girls are much too young for this!" she said crossly. "It's meant for married women only."

We needed a wider selection of magazines in order to sustain this fascinating hobby. Daddy subscribed to three—*Reader's Digest*, *Capper's Farmer*, and the *Farm Journal*. The first two were pretty useless. None was big on travel features. The *Farm Journal*, at least, included a section called "The Farmer's Wife," which contained fashion and grooming tips and offers for free recipes, detergent samples, and leaflets on stain removal. While searching the magazine, we discovered a column for teenage girls: "Dear Aunt Polly." This wise woman could remedy anything—pimples, big ears, small breasts, unruly hair, body odor, gossiping friends, and weary wardrobes. No problem was too large or small for her thoughtful, supportive response.

Peggy suggested we write a letter to "Dear Aunt Polly," just to see if she would answer. Maybe we could even get it published in the *Farm Journal*. The letter would have to be from Peggy; she was thirteen, a real teenager, entitled to some weighty problems. She didn't have any, of course, so we would have to invent something and try to make it sound believable.

How about this?

> Dear Aunt Polly,
>
> I am thirteen years old and I have twin sisters who are three years younger. They get all the attention, at home and at school, and everywhere we go.

Visiting Papa Willie's farm, summer 1953, Sara, Teddy, Priscilla, Peggy, and Susie (left to right)

"What do you think?" Peggy asked anxiously. "Does it sound sincere?"

"Sure!" said Susie. "But you'll have to make it more dramatic if it's going to get published. Let's say you are really starting to hate those twins."

Peggy looked away and frowned.

"Well, I agree," I told her. "It needs to sound really serious."

"Okay then, how about this?" Peggy continued to write:

> I know it's not their fault, but I am starting to hate them. My question is: How can I get over feeling so worthless and self-conscious? How can I make friends and get people to notice me?
>
> Please don't tell me to talk this over with anyone, because I just can't do that. I always start to cry. I hope you will print the answer in your magazine, but please don't use my real name or address.

"Awfully stupid, isn't it?" said Peggy. "Do you think she'll fall for it?"

"Well, sure . . . " We reached to hug her, but she pulled away, flustered and upset.

"I just made it up!" Peggy shouted. "You were the ones who wanted some more interesting mail. Maybe you can think of something better!"

"The letter is perfect," we assured her. "Don't change a single word."

We nearly ripped the June issue of Daddy's magazine out of its binding looking for "Dear Aunt Polly," but our letter wasn't there. A few days later Peggy received an envelope from the *Farm Journal*, addressed to "Miss Margaret Ann Hellerud." She rushed to her bedroom where she read it privately. When she finally came out, she refused to share.

"Was that really a letter from 'Dear Aunt Polly'? Did she take you seriously? What did she have to say?"

Peggy shrugged. "It was a dumb problem, so of course it was a dumb reply." Later on she said she lost the letter. She said she would try to remember what it said and tell us sometime, if we really had to know.

Peggy grew increasingly distant through the summer. She refused to allow us in her bedroom anymore and kept the door tightly closed even when she was not there. She peered around anxiously before scampering to the outhouse, as if it were a shameful mission. We, in turn, began snooping and spying. It did not take us long to find a major clue—a big box of Kotex hidden in her bottom dresser drawer.

We knew what it meant. The monthlies. The curse. We had learned all about it from the Kotex company. They had sent a free booklet—*You're a Young Lady Now*—that tried to make this humiliating problem sound like fun. It pictured teenage girls in ponytails and rolled-up dungarees talking on the telephone, lying on the floor with their feet propped on doorframes and windowsills. Peggy was never going to look like this, and neither were we. For one thing, we had no telephone. Our dungarees were baggy corduroys or barnyard denims. And I could not imagine what would happen if my sisters or I lounged in the doorways of our busy household. It could be dangerous.

Peggy was not acting as pleased as the book suggested she might. Besides getting the monthly cramps, she was breaking out in pimples all over her nose and forehead. When Peggy started eighth grade late in August, she hunched at the mirror above the washbasin, pushed and squeezed until the pimples were fiery red, then frantically buried them under gobs of pancake makeup as the school bus rumbled up the road.

Mama must have sympathized. She began taking special interest in Peggy's wardrobe, asking her what the young girls were wearing these days. Would she like to order penny loafers from the catalog? Of course, she would. She needed socks, too, with those big bulky cuffs, and a starchy petticoat.

"*Crinoline*, Mama," Peggy corrected, perking up considerably. "And a circle skirt. Not just a flarey skirt, but a big full circle, out to here." She flapped her arms to demonstrate.

Within a week Peggy had her stylish shoes and crinoline from

"Monkey Wards" and a bright-blue, flowered circle skirt fashioned on Mama's Singer. She pranced around the house, her perky hemline brushing the woodwork as she passed. Mama nodded her approval. Daddy wagged his head, trying not to smile.

At bedtime Peggy was still flying high. She invited Susie and me into her bedroom to admire the twirling skirt, and before we knew it we were locking arms, dancing joyful figure-eights around the room.

We barely heard Mama hollering over the commotion.

"Kids, stop that jumping! Your father needs his sleep."

We danced on tiptoe for awhile but were soon stomping out more figure-eights over our parents' heads.

"*Quiet!*" Daddy thundered.

We tried to simmer down but grew boisterous again, carried away by a bewildering excitement we could not control.

We did not hear his footsteps on the stairs and were completely startled when he burst into the room.

Peggy got it first. He had to fling her on the bed and yank up all those frilly petticoats in order to smack her bottom. She gave one sharp cry, then was stunned into silence as his broad hand cracked a dozen times against her plump buttocks. She lay still for several minutes afterward with her face pressed into the chenille bedspread, and when she rose her cheeks were flushed and mottled with white blossoms of remorse.

Susie went next. She refused to cry so her spanking lasted longer. I turned away and stared out the window. By the time my turn came, Daddy's rage was spent, and I got only a few half-hearted swats while I concentrated on a veil of wispy clouds sliding across the moon.

Daddy left without a word. Peggy snapped out the light. She stood a long time with her arms around our shoulders.

"My fault," she said, sounding remarkably composed.

We didn't move.

"Remember when we wrote that letter to Aunt Polly?" Peggy asked. "I didn't make the problem up. For years I've felt so inferior, so jealous of you twins . . . sometimes I thought I hated you." She raced through that confession, and still it tangled in her throat.

"What did she write to you?" we asked in unison.

"Her letter seemed so useless—I ripped it up. She said if I practiced thinking of others more than myself I could get over feeling self-conscious and shy. She said if I was kind and thoughtful everyone would want to be my friend."

"Of course they will, Peggy. Probably it just takes time—and practice."

"Well, I've been practicing. Right now I'm thinking about Daddy. He must be feeling pretty bad. Maybe if we go downstairs and say we're sorry . . . "

I did not want to go. For the first time ever, I felt clear, sharp anger toward my father. I wanted to hold onto it, build and shape it, somehow save it up for Peggy who was so defenseless and forgiving.

Susie and I followed her down the stairs. We found Daddy, slumped and defeated, in his parlor chair.

"We're sorry we made so much noise," Peggy began bravely, looking straight into his tired eyes. I murmured an apology, not feeling it at all.

"I'm sorry, too," Daddy whispered hoarsely. When he lifted his head, I saw the tear-stained cheeks.

I reached for a calloused hand. My sisters hugged his neck.

Peggy's circle of blue flowers spun quickly out of fashion. By fall the high school girls were wearing long, slim skirts that bound their legs so tight they had to shuffle through the hallways and move sideways up the stairs. Mama sewed up several sheaths for

Peggy, who wanted to be equally confined. She seemed to be making friends and gaining confidence.

Peggy passed the circle skirt along to her twin sisters, and we wore it out completely. After that the wilted garment lingered in our closet like a poplin bouquet.

Sheep

In 1953 I viewed the world through Daddy's eyes. Like him, I saw dairy cows as inept, demanding creatures. Ugly things, with knobby joints, sharp hipbones, drooling mouths, and twitching, ropey tails.

Sheep were soft and pliable. Dependent as cows, but quieter about it. Daddy liked their docile temperament. He liked the way they flocked together, the way they followed a leader with trust and obedience. He enjoyed the lambing season most of all, when the hours were longest, when his services were urgently required. That was late March to mid-April, a time of raw spring winds, cold rains, even tardy blizzards. The newborns must not be dropped on chilly ground where they might wander off or catch pneumonia. They must be nuzzled and nourished without delay, bonded by sight and scent to their natural mothers. Daddy worked around the clock at lambing time, penning the laboring ewes safely in the shed and assisting the precarious births. His watchfulness could not prevent all cases of ketosis, milk fever, hemorrhage, four-footed presentations, or twins who charged together down the narrow birth canal. There were always some maternal deaths with helpless orphans left to the shepherd's care.

Daddy made sunrise rounds to gather in the ewes who were coming near their time. Susie and I toured the pasture every afternoon. We knew the signs—a sway-backed, sunken appearance in front of the hipbones, a swelling udder, and a restless attitude. We were also armed with scientific data. All the sheep wore numbered ear tags. The ram was fitted with a marking harness during breeding in October, and a bright blue crayon marked the back of every ewe as she was mounted. Daddy noted all their due dates on the kitchen calendar for future reference.

Occasionally we missed a laboring ewe, and she delivered in the unprotected grassland. Daddy bundled the shivering lamb in his jacket, bore it home, and warmed it in a cardboard box beside the kitchen range.

The unlucky lamb might be disowned by its mother if she had not absorbed its scent during those crucial early hours. She often shoved it aside and refused to let it nurse her swollen teats. Twins and triplets also risked rejection. The ewe might bond with only one lamb or be lacking enough milk to feed a pair of eager sucklings. Orphaned lambs or "bummers" might be grafted to a freshly delivered ewe who had lost her own baby or had sufficient milk for doublets. But the shepherd must be quick and clever. The fetal fluids must be smeared over the orphan before bonding could occur. And the lamb must have colostrum to protect it from disease throughout its fragile infancy.

Daddy made valiant efforts to encourage these adoptions. Once we saw him skin the wrinkled coat from a dead baby and tie it to the body of a bleating orphan. The effort failed. Mothers were not easily deceived.

Freaks of nature were uncommon, but they did occur. One yearling gave birth to a woolly pillow with a well-formed head and tail but no sign of legs at all. There must have been internal blunders also, for the creature looked around, blatted twice, and died.

"Poor little duffer," said Daddy. "It's a blessing that he didn't last."

Daddy rubbed the moist warm torso against a recently rejected twin. This time he accomplished a graft with the lambless mother whose udder overflowed with milk.

This lambing game took skill. And luck. The timing was not always right. Every spring my sisters and I nourished several foundlings who demanded to be fed six times a day. They were intense and greedy, never fully satisfied. We cradled them in our laps at first. As they gained strength and size, we fed them through the woven wire fence that screened us from their clamoring hooves and searching mouths and fiercely sucking tongues. We held the long black nipples to the bottlenecks with firm, two-fisted grips. If our attention flagged for even a moment, the lamb would tug the tightly fitted nipple free, spilling warm cow's milk over hands and shoes, into the quack and clover.

We gave our bottle-babes capricious names like Corliss Archer or Amos, Andy, and Sapphire, after sassy characters we knew from radio. They grew plump and sturdy in a few exhausting weeks. We reduced the feedings to four times, then three, then twice a day, supplemented with grain and alfalfa until they were fully weaned and integrated with the flock. We watched them scamper in the pasture, frolic like children in a schoolyard playing tag and ring-around-the-rosy. They danced and leaped, came down on stiffened legs, and bounced across the pasture like smooth, white stones skipping over a grassy pond.

We had done our work well. We had raised our bummers up and set them free. We could hardly pick them out from their companions; yet they knew their keepers. The mere sound of our voices brought the orphans bounding expectantly across the meadow. They were bonded to us firmly for the remainder of their short but joyful lives.

Before the heat of summer settled in, we herded the new lambs into the sheep shed where Daddy docked their tails. The amputations looked cruel and bloody, but Daddy said the tails were more than a nuisance—they caused manure to soil the fleece. Blowflies laid their eggs in dirty tags of wool. We had seen the result: maggots infesting the rectum, devouring the tender innards. Advanced cases were difficult to treat and could mean a dreadful death.

One by one Daddy caught the frisky lambs and chopped their tails an inch from the base, using a dull knife that he claimed would cause less bleeding than a sharp one. They bled all the same. Daddy threw the severed tails aside into a growing heap of woolly worms. After docking the males, he castrated each one, using a wicked-looking pair of pliers especially designed for the job. The slimy testicles were tossed into a bucket that we did not inspect at closer range. The lambs cried piteously as they exited the gate and limped back to pasture. But in a day or two the ugly stumps showed signs of healing, and the lambs were playing carefree games again.

Shearing time was more to our liking. Peggy, Susie, and I hung on the sheep-shed gate like charmed Bo-Peeps, watching the ewes emerge from under Daddy's skillful electric clippers, small and shamed and naked. Daddy cradled the sheep between his legs and shifted them into a series of positions from which they seldom struggled to get free. He started shearing at the brisket, up into the left shoulder, keeping one knee behind the sheep's back, the other foot in front. Then he moved the clippers smoothly across the head and shoulders, down the back and rump and belly, finishing at the flanks and rear. Finally he shook the fleece free all in one fine piece, spread it skin side down upon the tarp, folded the edges inward, rolled and baled it up with twine, weighed it, and stuffed it into a sack.

By nightfall the burlap bags were bulging with wool, ready for market. It was a long but energizing day, and Daddy looked more pleased than tired.

"A fine crop," he declared with satisfaction. "Good clean wool! Bet these fleeces will average eleven pounds apiece." He held out his hands so we could stroke his palms and fingers, which were soft with lanolin.

Summer was barely beginning. The warmest months were treacherous; they offered up a host of ills that kept the shepherd constantly on guard. He fought internal parasites, drenching the flock with stout liquid medications, then shifted his sheep to unpolluted pastures. He watched for ticks and lice, for polio, coccidiosis, poison foliage, foot scald, bloat, and scours. When trouble struck, he intervened with drugs and pesticides and patience.

Dogs also posed a threat to the flock, especially in the summer months when the sheep ranged far from their protective shelter. This was one menace for which Daddy had no tolerance. He was outraged when he learned that a pack of canines had been marauding through the pasture and attacking his sheep, biting their shorn rumps and naked hocks. Fury turned to grief when he discovered three defenseless ewes had been chased down, bitten savagely, and disemboweled for the sheer sport of it.

Daddy stalked the pasture himself, and when he identified a German shepherd leading several smaller strays, he confronted its owner. The man refused to tie his dog, insisting it was innocent. A few days later Daddy saw his flock running in terror from the murderous pack. He killed the leader with a single shot, then buried him behind the barn. "There's no way to do right in this situation," he mourned aloud. No accusations or apologies followed the painful incident. To my knowledge, Daddy and his neighbor never spoke of it at all.

In early August Daddy helped us pick a few prize lambs for exhibition at the Polk County Fair. We seldom chose our bottle pets; they might be husky and handsome but were too playful to be handled in the ring. The show lamb required a solid stance, a blocky build, short neck, straight back, and even jaws and teeth. Daddy had an eye for winners. We washed and clipped and carded the chosen ones until they looked like blocks of snowy wool set

Susie (left) and Sara with a trio of yearling lambs at the Polk County Fair, August 1955

Harvey and Gus, the grand champion ram, 1955

on four round pegs. Daddy worked beside us, preparing his purebred Shropshire ram for competition. "Sheepmen claim 'the ram is half the flock,' and I can understand their thinking. This fellow has produced some mighty pretty lambs."

"He's nice and fat," I said in praise of the handsome animal.

"Yes—and I probably should cut back his grain, especially at breeding time. They say you have to get a ram down to his working clothes. But I like to keep this fellow happy."

Daddy named his ram Caesar Augustus and called him Gus for short. Our show lambs, too, had ancient, epic names—Brutus, Moses, Sampson, and Delilah.

We brought home ribbons, pinned them up on tagboard, and displayed them in the parlor. These stripes of color—blue and red and yellow and Gus's Grand Champion lavender—cheered us through the deep, white months ahead.

By late fall the ewes had grown a thick new fleece. The lambs weighed nearly ninety pounds. Daddy marked a few choice females for next year's breeding, then corralled the market lambs and culled the aging ewes for shipment to the stockyards in South St. Paul. Peggy, Susie, and I helped to chase them down, but we retreated to the house before the final loading. Our devoted orphans were usually aboard the truck when the gates slammed shut and the rig sped down the driveway, out of sight.

We never ate a single lamb chop in all those years that Daddy kept a flock. Although we grew tired of tough, stringy beef from wasted Holsteins, none of the shepherds thought of butchering a lamb. If Mama did, she was wisely silent.

Winter was a quiet time for the sheep as well as for their keepers. The flock blended into the frosted landscape. On stormy days the woolly creatures huddled in their darkened shelter. When I filled their mangers, I was greeted by a hundred quiet eyes glowing like blue jewels in the somber sky. At bedtime their low bleating was a winter lullaby.

Daddy was eager for signs of spring, yet he was grateful for this respite. "They don't need much attention in the winter. Just water, hay, and a little grain or corn silage. A simple shelter. Fellow could almost take a short vacation. I'd consider it, if it weren't for those milk cows. They never let you have a day of rest."

Daddy wondered aloud why everyone was milking Holsteins. Why weren't more sheep seen around this region? Managed properly, a flock could thrive on thin, rocky soil. He supposed that sheep were just too wide-ranging, maybe too agreeable to interest the average farmer, who wanted to be beaten down and held at home as only a dairy herd could do.

Oh, sure, he understood the appeal of dairying in Wisconsin, where nutritious grasses could be run through cows and converted into milk and cheese and butter and a steady income for the farmer. But as far as he could see, that was no way to live.

He did not need to explain it further. It was clear to me that my father was no dairy farmer. He felt crushed by a relentless march of ordinary days. But he could work with creatures who were calm and passive, yet demanding in their season.

I feared or pitied the tormented farmer when he was gripped by rage or bowed by despair. But I adored the shepherd when he gave his best, in bursts of pride and passion, to his sheep.

A Better Place

"Come, Boss, come, Boss," Mama sang in a high-pitched monotone. Thirty hulking Holsteins filed through the barn door, paraded down the freshly limed walk, entered their appointed stalls, and waited for Mama to click the stanchions shut around their slender necks. They stood obediently, slurping from their water cups, munching hay and silage from the trough until the milk had been sucked from their bulging udders. After milking was completed, Mama swung herself from stall to stall and set them free.

Daddy's impatient movements made the cattle restive and skittish. Mama calmed them, washing and massaging their udders, slipping the milkers on with speed and grace. When a sick or injured cow required manual stripping, Mama pulled her stool in close and stroked its flank. Her voice coaxed gently as her fingers pulled and squeezed the teats, pumping the milk into her pail in forceful streams. The critter seldom kicked or bellowed.

Heads turned as Mama passed. She was director of a dense arena, humid with heaving breath, fermented corn, raw milk, steaming urine and manure. She was quick and confident. The cattle knew she was in firm control; Daddy knew it, too.

Mama organized the players, called the scenes:

"Better keep Bertha in tonight. She's feverish, and she didn't touch her feed—I'll bet her gut has been punctured by a nail or another length of baling wire. Let's get the vet to put a magnet in her belly to collect that hardware since she seems so fond of it."

"Looks like Mary stepped on a teat—we'll have to watch her for mastitis."

"Doris is coming into heat. Let's pen her with the bull tomorrow morning—those young heifers can be hard to settle."

She gave reviews and terminations.

"Time we shipped poor Aggie off to South St. Paul. Her production has been low all year, and now she's showing signs of lump jaw."

"Not bad—overall—considering we don't have a purebred herd. This month they averaged eighty pounds of milk apiece per day. They're getting twenty pounds of ensilage, ten pounds of hay, and eight of grain, just what the county agent recommends. It's paying off. Our butterfat is testing three-point-five percent."

Daddy provided the muscle. He hoisted ninety-pound cans of milk down the barn walk into the cooler and wrestled them out of the cold water every morning when the milk truck came. During winter Daddy climbed the icy silo rungs and chipped out frozen silage for the herd, which stayed five months inside the barn. He cleaned the gutters daily, shoveling wet hay and manure into a barrow, wheeling it out, and heaping it on a frozen mountain in the barnyard. He would mine that mountain in the spring, move it scoop by scoop into the spreader and scatter it across the fields. Fifteen tons of rich manure was dumped each year by every thousand pounds of animal, half of it landing in the barn during the confining winter months, to be carted out and plowed into the soil.

It was crushing, relentless labor.

Steady, Mama called it. No fear of unemployment. Reliable income. Sheep paid off only twice a year—one crop of wool, one crop of lambs. Cows produced a milk check every month unless you dried your herd in winter. That was no way to farm, she said, not in Wisconsin where you had to house and feed the cattle throughout the winter. You had to maximize your profits by staggering the breeding, maintaining some production year around. Best to have several freshening in autumn when the price of milk rose due to dwindling supply. Even then it would not pay, not without acreage that could produce lush pasture and nutritious corn and oats and hay.

Our rocky, sandy farm at Balsam Lake was marginal, broken up by creeks and ponds and sloughs, forested hills, mysterious craters banked with wild columbine. It was a joy to kids with toboggans and fishing poles. A refuge for birds and wildlife. Acceptable to sheep, whose cleft lips and narrow noses fitted them for meager pickings.

A herd of Holsteins needed more. Mama found it for them.

In the fall of 1953 we moved ten miles, to a farm just south of Milltown. It was flat and nearly treeless, like Nebraska prairie; we

"A Better Place"—the Hellerud farm south of Milltown, about 1960

might as well have gone a thousand miles. There was scarcely a tree on the entire one hundred acres. The soil was rich and dark with no roots or boulders waiting for an unsuspecting plow.

"You won't be harvesting any rocks from that field!" Mama exclaimed, slipping her arm around Daddy's waist as they surveyed the dark soil running south of the barnyard, smooth and unbroken, more than half a mile.

"Nope."

"No stumps to blast, no treacherous hills to climb on the John Deere. Remember when you overturned the tractor going into that steep hollow? I thought I'd lost you."

"You almost did," he said.

For five kids who had loved their wild places, there was little to celebrate. We did applaud some features of the big, square farmhouse. A telephone, at last. A bathtub, running water. Five spacious bedrooms, four up, one down; only Susie and I would have to share. The house had been badly shaken by a tornado, evidenced by jagged cracks in walls and ceilings. That didn't worry Mama; she was already planning the repairs. An old barn and several sheds had been destroyed completely.

The rebuilt barn was sixty feet long, half again as large as the weary, weathered structure on the Balsam Lake farm. There were two long rows of stanchions, fifteen on each side, with calf pens and box stalls on the south end, feed room and adjacent silo on the north. The gutters were deep, fitted with a chain conveyor for moving the manure. The hayloft, which soared thirty-two feet, was braced by massive timbers, diagonally boarded to withstand heavy winds. The milk house was poorly situated and ill equipped. It would not meet the Land O' Lakes Grade A requirements, but Mama hoped to add a modern bulk tank later. That was the coming thing, and it would be a great convenience: no more hoisting ninety-pound cans of milk in and out of the water cooler, no more twisted backs and busted knees. In the meantime, they could sell Grade B milk to Stella Cheese in Milltown for $2.90 per hundredweight. Since Milltown was only one mile away, Daddy could take the cans to town himself and save on hauling fees.

Susie and I shared a bedroom directly over our parents', and their bedtime conversations funneled through the furnace duct directly to our ears. Sometimes they were too tired to talk at all. But a few weeks after the move, we were startled by an argument that lasted for a miserable half hour.

"It was a damned good move!" Mama was saying. "Twelve thousand dollars for this place, compared with ten for those hills and swamps at Balsam Lake!"

"What if we can't sell the Balsam place? We can't continue farming both of them."

"Then we'll sell it in pieces—the buildings are almost worthless anyway. Farmers will be expanding, looking for connecting land. We'll all have to farm bigger and smarter if we want to survive this game."

"I'm not sure I want to survive it. And it burns me that your dad financed us. I know he's a helluva farmer. He knows how to suck money from a herd of Holsteins better than anyone for miles around. But I'm not Willie Williamson! I'm not a cattle man. No one seems to think about my needs."

"What *are* your needs, Harvey?"

"By God, Helen, I wish I knew. My folks weren't farmers like the Williamsons, so none of this comes naturally to me."

"What does come naturally to you? This is dairy country, Harvey."

"For Christsake, Helen! There are other places in the world besides Polk County and work more satisfying than those stinking cows!" His voice was hoarse with anger and despair. Huddled by the hot-air register, Susie and I began to cry. We wadded the skirts of our flannel nighties and pressed them to our mouths to stifle the sound, but our parents must have heard because their talking stopped abruptly.

Within minutes Mama entered our room with a sack of marshmallows she had warned us not to pilfer from the pantry. She stuffed the soft, plump treats into our open mouths.

"Don't, Twins, please don't cry. This is a better place for all of us. Daddy will see that, too, real soon. Everything will be all right. Now go to sleep."

Mama forgot her marshmallows. She left the entire twelve-ounce package lying open on the pillow near our heads.

Our parents prospered on the Milltown farm. The summer of 1954 brought bumper crops, enabling Mama and Daddy to purchase ten more top-grade Holsteins, filling every stanchion in the barn. At eight years old Teddy was an eager herdsman, rising at six o'clock each day to help with chores. We older girls were glad to see our pesky little brother had been born to some purpose; he would save us from future service in the barn. We cooked and cleaned and washed and ironed, all without complaint, and seldom ventured out except to call the farmers in for supper.

We often saw our mother standing in the barnyard, hand cupped around her mouth: "Come, Boss, come, Boss . . . "

It was their mealtime, too. The cows would munch fresh hay and grain while we ate beef stew in the farmhouse kitchen, made from the carcasses of barren heifers or aged culls who had no more to give.

"Why do you call them 'Boss'?" I asked at the supper table. I had heard the call so many years; now, suddenly, I wondered what it meant.

"Because they are the boss—they run our lives," said Daddy sourly.

"No, Harvey," Mama explained patiently. "I studied Latin years ago, in high school, and if I recall correctly, the word bos—spelled b o s—means ox, or cow."

"What do you like so much about those clumsy, smelly animals?" I teased.

She took the question seriously. "The calves are beautiful. So is the sound of fresh milk poured into the strainer, raining down inside the hollow can. And the cows—well, they're *reliable*. Creatures of habit. They need a regular schedule, a familiar place. They'll always seek the same stall, and that's important, so you always milk them from the same position, always left or always right. They need to hear the same voices and feel the same careful, reassuring hands. That's why you don't want strangers handling your herd. Safety and security, that's all they ask. And no surprises."

Mama needed safety; Daddy liked surprises. As long as they milked Holsteins, there would be no compromise.

Party Line

The new farmhouse was a thirty-foot-square, white clapboard structure set on a cement foundation. The clean, efficient oil furnace in the basement never belched or backfired. Warm air flowed evenly to every room. The small, downstairs bathroom contained a flushing toilet, a wall-hung sink with hot and cold running water, and—best of all—a deep, claw-footed tub. Mama was so accustomed to conserving precious water that she never allowed us to draw more than four or five inches. The hot water cooled quickly as it hit the porcelain, and I bruised my elbows and shoulder blades trying to submerge my body in the shallow, lukewarm bath. After years of longing for the luxury of indoor plumbing, this was a major disappointment.

As far as I could tell, our biggest gain from this traumatic move was the telephone, which allowed us to converse with friends and neighbors whenever we pleased. The varnished wooden box was mounted on a wall just inside the kitchen door. It was fitted with twin bells, round and silver, like a pair of bulging eyes. A long, black snout in the center held the mouthpiece. The side panels featured a pair of mismatched ears: a cone-shaped receiver dangled on the left, a small black crank protruded on the right. One turn of that crank could connect us to friends and neighbors all over Polk County, and beyond.

Our ring was long-long-short-long, and it brought Helleruds running from all four corners of the house. Most of the calls were from our Williamson relatives or our new neighbors, who always asked for Mama. She was obviously enjoying the telephone. We noticed how she smoothed her hair and tucked in her blouse as if her callers could spy right through the snout. Gradually Susie, Peggy, and I began receiving calls from our new schoolmates, who rang us up to check a math assignment or ask what we might be wearing to school the following day.

Ours was a party line, and we soon recognized thirteen other calls as well. Short-long-long belonged to the Holms, a half mile down the road. That signal tempted us to listen. Mrs. Holm was an eager gossip who kept up with everyone's affairs. The Hendricksons (three shorts and a long) had two teenage daughters with ardent boyfriends calling every evening. Peggy covered the mouthpiece with a wadded dishtowel and listened to the teasing and sighing, hoping to pick up a few pointers on the courting game.

Long-short-long was Oscar Swenson's ring. We soon ignored his calls, which were usually from an elderly sister complaining of lumbago or the contrary weather. Oscar did his share of eavesdropping, though. A widower who milked his small herd at 5:00 P.M., he spent long evenings tuning in to his neighbors. He had a creaky rocking chair and a grandfather clock that ticked loudly and chimed every quarter hour. We always knew when Oscar Swenson was hanging on the line.

A sequential ringing of all fourteen parties meant that Mrs. Reynolds was gathering material for her weekly social column in the *Milltown Advertiser.* A curious neighbor could hear the news before it made the paper—and some that wasn't fit to publish.

Mama warned us sternly against eavesdropping.

"The telephone is for business, not a toy, not meant for idle gossip."

Whenever we lifted the receiver and heard voices on the line, we were expected to hang up promptly and await our turn. We teased Mama when she seemed reluctant to hang up herself. Sometimes she placed her hand over the mouthpiece and whispered frantically: "Hush, kids! They'll be winding up any minute, and I don't want to lose my chance."

I wondered to myself why it was called a "party line." It was no party waiting for that line when you really needed it. It could be pretty irritating.

Mama got annoyed, too, every time she opened the monthly phone bill. "This service fee is just outrageous! Two-eighty! It ought to be divided fourteen ways. Twenty cents would be about right, considering how long I have to wait for my share of the line."

Sometimes she had to interrupt when she was standing in her barn boots, waiting for the line to clear so she could call the vet. "Excuse me, ladies. Would you mind continuing your conversation later? We have a critter about to throw her womb."

Everyone understood that request, and they usually rang off without delay. One at a time the receivers lifted again as the good neighbors confirmed that the interruption was justified.

In order to reach the vet, Mama had to call the central operator (one short ring) and ask to be connected to Doc Wilson. Fortunately the vet had a private line all to himself. If he could not be found at home, "Central" usually knew his whereabouts and would ring that farm instead.

Susie and I eventually made friends with another fifth grader named Trudee, whose mother was the daytime Central in the Milltown office. One day after school Trudee marched us right into the telephone company, past the receptionist, and into the back room where her plump, golden-haired mother was working the switchboard. She resembled an organist seated at a console. Her nimble hands were flipping the cables up and down, jacking them in and out in all directions. Trudee's mother nodded and smiled in greeting, pointing to the earphones, the mouthpiece by way of apology.

"Central."

"That party line is busy—please try again."

"An emergency? Please hold on, I'll interrupt for you."

"We need to clear this line for a few minutes. The doctor needs to get through. Thank you."

"Central."

"Your mother isn't home right now, Bobby. I think you'll find her at your Aunt Margie's house. Do you want me to ring her there?"

"Central."

"The Curtis Hotel in Minneapolis? Just a minute while I connect you with the long-distance operator."

"Cum-on," said Trudee. "She's always too busy to talk at this time of day."

Central smiled and waved without missing a beat, playing chords of conversation that wrapped around the world.

The Blacksmith

Susie and I settled quickly into our new classroom at Milltown Elementary in the fall of 1953. We enjoyed instant popularity as the only pair of identical twins in the entire school. We were eager fifth-grade scholars. Miss Olva Johnson, a gentle, blue-haired spinster in her sixties, was fond of poetry. Longfellow, Whitman, Sandburg, Frost. The class memorized dozens of poems and chanted them together like a choir. One of our favorites was Henry Wadsworth Longfellow's tribute to "The Village Smithy":

Under a spreading chestnut-tree
The village smithy stands;
The smith, a mighty man is he,
With large and sinewy hands;
And the muscles of his brawny arms
Are strong as iron bands.

His hair is crisp, and black, and long,
His face is like the tan;
His brow is wet with honest sweat,
He earns whate'er he can,
And looks the whole world in the face,
For he owes not any man . . .

By 1953 there were few horses around anymore, yet Milltown still had its timber blacksmith shop and a smithy standing in its open doorway. His name was Martin P. Michaelson. He had been a professional wrestler in his youth, a huge, strong man who wrestled all over the country. But he married a local girl, Helena Lindvig, and they settled down. For Martin that settling meant fifty years of swinging sledges, mending plows, and shoeing horses, an exacting trade no pioneer town could do without. All that—yet Martin never talked about himself, seldom talked at all. We knew some stories, though. The blacksmith's strength and stamina were legendary. On Christmas Day, 1917, an electrical fire started in the basement of Milltown Lutheran Church, and the beautiful Gothic structure burned to the ground. It was Martin Michaelson who carried out prized furnishings and fixtures and rescued the larger-than-life statue of Christ, carrying it to safety as the blazing roof collapsed behind him. Folks still described the scene thirty-six years later.

Martin was a hulking man, with deep, sad eyes. Nearly retired, he mended nothing more important than a child's wagon or a bicycle fender now and then. School kids loitered near the shop, peeked in the doors and windows, wondering what might be stored inside. Occasionally someone asked for a demonstration. That was when he sprang to life.

"You see this forge—it's three foot square, brick and stone and made to last. Hollow underneath so I can dump the fire and get the ashes out, like so. Those bellows overhead pump in the air I need to keep the fire hot. Chimney has a twelve-inch flue for plenty of draught. Each hammer has a special purpose. This here's a tapping hammer, with a stone head . . . twist hammer . . . dog-head hammer . . . crossface—good for straightening saws."

Susie and I knew just enough to make us curious about Martin and his shop. He was a relative of sorts; his only daughter Ethel had married Mama's eldest brother Raymond, who had drowned in the Apple River a year after we were born. The adults still talked about the tragedy at family gatherings when they thought the kids had all run out to play.

"Thank God for those twins—I don't know how the folks could have survived that year without them. Remember—even Martin came on Sunday afternoons to share their loss and always wound up bouncing those toddlers on his lap."

He did not recognize us as we passed, and we were glad somehow. One autumn afternoon we saw Martin lounging against the shop door, cap pulled low over his forehead, thumbs twisted in his belt loops, hitching his pants halfway up to his armpits. We dared each other to approach him.

"Why did you want to be a blacksmith, Martin? How did you

Main Street, Milltown, Wisconsin, 1958

learn the trade? How many horses could you shoe in a day? Did you fix sleds and buggies? What happened once the farmers all got cars and tractors?"

After three or four eager questions, Martin invited us inside the blacksmith shop. It was black, all right. Like Martin himself, the building was permanently stained with soot and grime. Bolts and spikes, scraps of tin, bits of leather harness lay scattered on the hard earth floor. There was no place to sit; we stood near Martin as he pointed out his tools.

"Vice-bench, with a drawer for taps and eyes. This here's a wheelhorse . . . I still repair a cartwheel now and then. Tongs, calipers, and chisels . . . used to have a rack of them. Four men working at one time. We kept a steady pace. Always fired with top-grade coal. Cumberland. Burns quick, gives off strong, steady heat. Bought this anvil fifty years ago from a retiring smithy in St. Paul."

"What's this called, Martin? And this?"

"Trip hammer . . . band saw . . . drilling machine . . . powered by this six-horsepower gasoline engine. Sheering sharpener . . . the best a man can buy."

Week in, week out, from morn till night,
You can hear his bellows blow;
You can hear him swing his heavy sledge,
With measured beat and slow,
Like a sexton ringing the village bell,
When the evening sun is low . . .

Martin's shop stood on the north side of Main Street, between Miller Hardware and the Milltown State Bank. The timber walls stood straight and strong through five decades of wind and sleet and snow, but the brick chimney was tumbling now, and the roof was caving. It was a narrow building, dark and deep. Rays of sunlight slanted through the open bifold doors and two small, cracked windowpanes. The fire in the forge must have added precious light during the fifty years that Martin worked within those dingy walls.

The forge was cold in 1953. Yet there was coal in the box and water in the cooling trough. In its dying days, Martin's shop was still equipped for work. A visitor standing in the open doorway almost expected to hear the anvil ring, the bellows blow.

And children coming home from school
Look in at the open door;
They love to see the flaming forge,
And hear the bellows roar,
And catch the burning sparks that fly
Like chaff from a threshing-floor . . .

Throughout that year my twin and I stopped to chat with Martin whenever we were in town. He grew more talkative with every visit, and yet he never seemed to notice we were a matched pair and never asked our names. We sensed he did not need to know us, only craved an audience so he could talk about his work and make it come to life again.

One Saturday morning he described the Milltown of his youth, boasted that smithing kept him busy six days out of seven during those rousing, robust years. He calculated how many thousands of horseshoe nails he had pounded in his lifetime, how many wheels and hitches, plows, and planters he had made and mended.

He fetched an old photo album from his house next door and showed us pictures of Main Street when Milltown was a pioneer village. It looked like the set for a western movie with crude, low buildings, muddy tote roads, sidewalks built of wooden planking, horses and buggies everywhere.

"Population was about three hundred when I built this shop in 1902. Town has nearly doubled now, but there's nowhere near the commotion we had back then. Yep, those were the days," said Martin.

How things had changed. Even John Miller's hardware store was struggling to stay in business. Everyone owned a fast car these days. Folks could drive all the way into the city looking for a better deal. Taverns were still thriving, though. Taverns and churches. He guessed we would have those, long after the local merchants closed their doors.

They tore down that old blacksmith shop in 1965, as soon as Martin could be persuaded to sell it to the village. His house next door went with it. Everyone agreed it was an eyesore, obsolete and shabby, right there on Main Street. It made a mighty poor impression for the tourists.

The bulldozer brought down bricks and timber and debris in one brief afternoon. Soon a smooth, asphalt parking lot paved over every trace of the structure, leaving no clues or questions for young scholars passing by.

Weather

April 21, 1939
Dear Mugsy [Mama's sister],

We've been on the farm three weeks today, and I find myself liking it first rate, as I knew I would. I've never been as happy or excited over anything as I am over farming with Harvey. He's so enthusiastic and ambitious, and such an early bird that I find myself wanting to get going early too. Harvey gets up between five and five-thirty, and I have been rolling out at six or shortly after. I think that's pretty good for a natural sleepy-head, don't you? I'm ready to go to bed when night comes, though, which is as it should be. When I get caught up on my house work I'm going to start taking a nap every afternoon and see if I can't gain back some of my lost weight. I have gained two pounds already, and now weigh two pounds more than our dog. No kidding—we have a dog here that weighs 96 pounds. He's a big black sheep dog named Pete, and he and looks for all the world like a big black bear. He practically eats us out of house and home, but he belongs to Harvey's uncle, so we're almost obliged to keep him on. He's not much good around the cattle either.

In addition to an over-grown, good-for-nothing dog, we have about 16 cows, some calves, pigs (7 new little pink ones just born the other day), 5 horses, 165 chickens, and 400 little ones coming in a couple weeks.

Harvey has also made himself a tractor, something like the one the boys rigged up at home. He calls it his "Thunderbug"—and does it ever live up to the name! We painted it green one day last week—Harvey says so he can hide in the tall grass while the other "real" tractors go by. It's not as funny looking as all that, though. In fact, Harvey is pretty *proud of it. It cost him only about $125, and it will do the work of a regular tractor and serve his purpose very well. He went out in the field the other day to see how it was going to work, but got stuck in the mud, so he decided he'd have to wait a few more days until it dried off a little. Then we got a big rain last Sunday and a snowstorm Monday that is just melting away today, so it will be about another week before Harvey can venture out and really give the thing a trial. He hauls cream to town with it, and can go along the highway about 30 or 40 miles an hour.*

Love,

Helen

Helen and the Thunderbug tractor, 1939

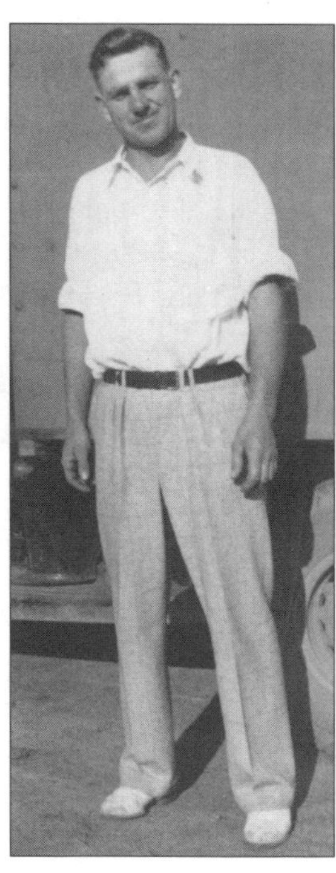

Harvey, about 1939

August 7, 1939
Dear Mugsy,

We are nearly finished with the threshing. Have one field of late oats left that will have to wait another week or so. We have a second crop of hay to put in—then filling the silo and plowing—but there won't be the mad rush that we've had all summer. We just finished haying and then had to start harvesting, so had no breathing space at all. I rode the binder and bumped the bundles for Harvey because he used the Thunderbug. It went ever so much faster than with horses, and since he had to do all the shocking too, the time saved was a help. We had 37 acres of grain—about the same amount they have on the home place. It was better than average this year, and we had an unusually good hay crop too, so will come out well on the feed for winter.

I've gotten tan as an Indian and am really quite the farmer now. I thought I knew a lot about the farm before, but never realized half of the work and effort that was put forth until I had a crack at it myself. Harvey likes it first rate, for which I'm more than glad. Life's too short to be doing something you don't really like, I think.

Love,

Helen

May 3, 1954
Dear Mugsy,

Our prolonged wet spell this spring was much needed and makes the prospects for this year much brighter. We had such a dry fall and hardly any snow this winter, so there was absolutely no moisture in the subsoil to carry us along in case of a dry spring. We had chances to rent our Balsam Lake land but decided against it and are cropping it ourselves. We have 30 acres ready to put into grain. The rest is in hay. If we have a good season the place will show up better than last year and our chances for selling it will be better. When we listed it last fall things were dry and nothing looked as good as it really was.

Harvey has had a bad sinus cold for two weeks—in fact, he did have to go to bed for a couple days. This cold, damp weather doesn't help. I think when the sun finally comes out and he starts working in these nice flat fields, things will go along better and he will perk up. Doing chores all winter tires a guy out and this is a terribly unhandy barn to work in.

If Harvey doesn't feel he wants to continue next fall, we will have to make a change—and I can't imagine what that might be—but I think he should give this place one year anyway before he makes up his mind. I talked to Papa about it, and he doesn't see how Harvey and I can miss with this good flat land. But of course we'll have to work together. We can't be heading off in separate directions.

Love,

Helen

In 1954 I knew my parents were pulling against each other. I also understood something of the reasons behind their differences. Mama was descended from the tenacious, hardworking Norwegian immigrants who had settled in Eureka Township, west of Milltown. She had grown up with dairy farming and accepted—almost welcomed—its constraints. She eagerly embraced the farm routine and the structured life it offered: busy days that turned on steady seasons, measured years.

Daddy had been reared in town. His mother, Agnes, was Danish, as were most other residents of the village. His father, Henry Hellerud, had been a schoolmaster in western Minnesota before he moved to Milltown in 1909 to serve as depot agent for the Soo Line Railroad, an important position in the thriving pioneer town. The Hellerud home was located only two blocks from the tracks. Young Harvey and his sister, Wanda, heard the whistling locomotives and saw the trains transporting passengers and parcels, bawling livestock, coal and oil, and the U.S. Mail in and out of Milltown several times each day.

Occasionally Agnes and her children traveled on their Soo Line passes, once riding as far west as Ogden, Utah, to visit relatives. That trip offered Harvey a tantalizing glimpse of the varied landscapes that stretched beyond the fields and fences of Wisconsin. He loved the western mountains and the wide, flat prairies of Dakota. He longed to visit distant towns and cities, western ranches and towering Pacific pines. It seemed illogical to settle for the life at hand without exploring the alternatives.

Harvey was also a cautious, modest man. As a child, he had received little warmth or praise from either parent. Lacking in self-confidence, he was not inclined to take unnecessary chances. The Great Depression further squelched his wanderlust and modified his prospects. His father urged him to try farming. Even if he could afford a college education, there was almost no employment to be found. Best he establish himself on a small farm here at home. It did not take much to get started in those days, and at least there would always be food on the table.

It made sense to him in 1934. Twenty years later, with a growing family to support, Harvey knew he had make a grave mistake. He was indentured to his hundred acres and a barn full of cattle. Day after dreaded day he milked the cows, scooped and pitched and spread manure, picked rocks, plowed, planted, cultivated, and gathered in the harvest. It was a crushing, endless cycle, allowing no vacations, not a single day of peace or rest. He saw no possibility of travel or a liberating education, now or ever.

My father missed his Balsam Lake farm with its swamps and trees and wildlife. While this bald, flat Milltown land might turn a better profit, it spoke to him of constant, regimented work. He could only blame himself; he had agreed to make the move, expand the dairy herd, and reduce his flock of sheep. It made economic sense, of course. He could not argue that.

After the move to Milltown, Daddy's temper flared with the slightest provocation. His hard-set jaw and heavy silences warned us when a storm was brewing. We ran for cover as the furious storm sucked him up, then flung him down and left him cursing and flailing. It did not occur to us to feel abused or angry when we were caught in the maelstrom and unfairly punished for some oversight or minor accident. We simply tried to lie as low as possible, hoping to minimize the damage and regrets.

One summer afternoon in 1954, when Mama was in town, Susie and I decided to surprise her with a batch of oatmeal cookies. We were untidy bakers. Daddy saw our mess when he came stomping in, fuming that the Allis Chalmers had broken down, leaving several acres of first-crop hay cut down and exposed to threatening weather. He scowled to see the dirty bowls and mixing spoons and eggshells heaped in the kitchen sink. His eyes followed the trail of sugar and flour from the open bins, across the linoleum floor, onto the pressback chairs, and over the checkered oilcloth protecting the tabletop.

"We're going to clean it up right now!" we assured him. "Here, Daddy—have a cookie—take a handful—they're still warm from the oven."

He slammed his fist down on the floury tabletop. "Christ Almighty! Do you have to make a goddamn mess as soon as Mama's back is turned? We work our asses off, and all you can do is make trouble! You good-for-nothing lazy louts—you don't do enough around here to wad a shotgun!" His raging words hurt more than any spanking.

We cleaned up quickly and were careful not to say a word to Mama, who wondered why our cookies stayed in the crock until they were hard and dry as little stones.

Daddy never lost his temper with the sheep, even when they strayed through a stretch of sagging fence and wound up gorging themselves in the corn or clover. But the cattle were a different matter. They quickly provoked his wrath. He could hardly tolerate these brutes who spooked so easily and were too stupid to find their own stanchions. They ingested hardware, stepped on their neighbors' teats, and sought shelter under tall trees during lightning storms. "If that wouldn't make a preacher swear!" Daddy yelled in a voice that went careening toward the sky.

Herding cattle was a dreaded chore for all of us—an invitation to a painful rampage. We knew our father's touchy disposition. And we knew well how nervous and excitable the cattle could be, especially in midsummer when they were plagued by deerflies and hot, sullen weather. But the job must be done. There was much rounding up and moving of cattle during those first summers on the Milltown farm. The Balsam farm had not yet sold, and so its distant pastures were still utilized for grazing young stock. On one occasion, when Mama, Peggy, Susie, and I were helping to move some heifers back to the Milltown farm, we had a terrible time getting them corralled. After much chasing, stomping, shouting, and waving, most of the heifers were funneled through the narrow gate and into the waiting truck. One young critter named Beauty refused to move despite our desperate efforts.

Daddy swore. He managed to lasso the heifer and tried to drag her through the gate. Frightened, she dug in with all four hooves and would not budge. Daddy threw the squalling animal to the ground, bound her legs together with loops of baling twine, and tied her to the rear bumper of his pickup parked nearby. Mama screamed in protest, but the engine roared above her cries while Daddy dragged the heifer over ruts and rocks and brambles. When the truck finally stalled in a gully, Beauty's hide was raw and torn and bloody. Daddy looked at her, astonished, as if he wondered what had brought her down.

Somehow they got Beauty home, and Mama doctored the animal herself; she did not see how she could call the vet and explain those injuries. Daddy retreated to the milk house for hours, and Mama made several trips with food and Thermoses of tea.

"Is Daddy sick?" I worried. Mama assured me he would be all right, but he was tired and needed a vacation.

On the tenth of August, after an early threshing, Daddy boarded the train and headed west to visit his cousin's stock ranch near Kaycee, Wyoming. This was extraordinary. He had never gone away before, not for more than a few hours between milkings. Now he planned to leave us for days or weeks, without a round-trip ticket.

Mama promised us that Daddy would be back—no doubt of that —but she counted on our willing help to keep things going in the meantime. Peggy would be needed in the barn to help stanchion the cows, pitch hay, scrape walks, feed calves, and empty buckets. Teddy was old enough to do errands and keep an eye on the milk strainer. Susie and I were charged with keeping house, weeding the garden, and minding four-year-old Prissy.

Within a few days we had mastered our routines and felt proud of our important contributions. Daddy's letters from Wyoming were increasingly hopeful, and he figured he would be home shortly after Labor Day.

"These ranchers say a lot of trees make them feel claustrophobic—they like their wide horizons—but I still crave some rolling hills and hardwoods."

A little later: "Lloyd has a big spread out here, but stock ranching has its own problems. He's lost cattle to rustlers three years running, and his sheep were plagued this year by lungworm. It's dry here, too. Compared to this country, Wisconsin is mighty *green*, even in a bad spell like we had last fall—so green it almost chokes you . . . "

His telegram arrived soon after that: DEAR HELEN HAD ENOUGH STOP MISS YOU AND THE KIDS STOP COMING SEPTEMBER TENTH 2 PM TRAIN MILLTOWN DEPOT STOP LOVE H3

Mama let all five of us go with her to meet Daddy's train, which thundered into the station exactly on schedule. He stepped down from the coach, squinted in the sunlight, and looked around as if he had disembarked in a strange, new place. Then he gathered us into his arms and held us a long time.

The Last Threshing

A sharply focused, black-and-white snapshot captures Teddy and me playing near the weathered granary. I know the bullthistles, the tall quack, the curving tines of a hayrake parked in the left corner. I know the hulking metal monster that stands in the background. This is the threshing machine—a Nichols and Shepard Red River Special. It stands fifteen feet tall and measures forty-five feet head to tail, from the front-end feeder housing to the bonnet on the blower pipe. Its spike-toothed cylinders can digest a field of oats in one voracious afternoon. This is a dinosaur on the eve of its extinction. The photograph is dated on the back—August 1955—the season of our last threshing.

This threshing beast knew many fields and many masters. It was too costly and cumbersome for one farmer to own and oper-

Seven Helleruds—Helen and Harvey behind Teddy, Priscilla, Sara, Susie, and Peggy—in 1954

ate. Neighbors pooled their labor and resources, buying one machine to serve eight or ten farms. As summer waned, they gathered around someone's kitchen table and drew up a schedule as fairly and sensibly as possible.

"Let's see, Ed, you were first last year so we'll have to put you further down the line."

"Lyle's oats are nearly ripe, and his shocks stood through three hard rains last year—we ought to start with him."

Each prayed for fine weather when the creature came lumbering onto his land. The cutting, binding, and shocking had been done in advance; golden tepees of oats stood pitched in the field, dry and ripe and ready for the final phase of harvest.

Now, from sunup to sundown the bundles were hauled in and fed to the ravenous machine, which rumbled and groaned as it separated the precious kernels from their dry, dusty stems. Chaff and straw were spit high into the air, raining down all day to form a shiny golden stack. The precious straw would serve as bedding for the cattle throughout their long winter confinement in the barn.

We girls were not allowed to hang around the noisy, dangerous equipment. Little Priscilla, only five, was not allowed outdoors at all. Yet our brother at the age of nine ran freely behind the wagons and perched on the fender of the laboring John Deere tractor that powered the giant machine. We girls kept busy in the kitchen all morning, peeling tubs of potatoes and carrots, snapping beans, stirring jugs of Kool-Aid, setting the table for ten hungry men who would appear promptly when the noon whistle blew in town.

It was a hearty, hasty feast, not long on conversation. When the crew had emptied their plates and pushed their chairs back from the table, there were piles of dirty dishes, pots, and pans to wash and dry. No time for lunch or recess. We nibbled on the leavings as we cleaned up the mess. Mama warned us to be quick—it was nearly time to prepare afternoon lunches. Sandwiches and fresh fruits and cake and hand-squeezed lemonade must be boxed and bagged and toted to the fields by three o'clock.

This picnic was our favorite part of threshing day. The men relaxed under a shade tree and shared a round of ethnic jokes—in which the Norwegians generally got the best of the poor dumb

Swedes—and some good-natured teasing and horseplay. Peggy, Susie, and I were noticed for the first time all day. ("How tall and pretty those girls are getting to be! And such a good help in the kitchen. They'll make fine farm wives some day, no doubt about that!")

With luck and fair weather, the oats were stored safely in the bins by twilight, and the sweaty crew was gone, tending to their own pressing chores at home. The threshing rig was hauled off down the road and readied for its next assignment.

When it was all over Daddy sank into his favorite chair without bothering to empty the cuffs of his overalls or brush away the chaff that had settled on his bushy brows.

"It was a bumper crop, a good ninety bushels to the acre," he reported on threshing night, 1955, "and it went like clockwork. Will you look at that strawstack! That's got to be the highest stack of good clean straw this farm has ever seen!"

It seemed to me he said that every year. Daddy always took great satisfaction in bringing in a healthy crop of oats. The strawstack stood like a gigantic monument to his achievement. Two years before—in 1953, when I was ten and Teddy seven—we celebrated by climbing to the top of the slippery mountain and flinging ourselves down, over and over again, until the stack was pocked with craters.

Daddy had been furious. "Damn it to hell!" he had exploded. "That strawstack wasn't settled! You kids have torn it up so bad—the rain will run straight through and *rot the whole damn stack!*"

He hadn't spanked us, although we certainly deserved it. The look on his face served as my punishment. I would never make that kind of mischief again, and I would see that Teddy didn't, either.

Daddy was gone right after milking to join the crew at Vollrath's farm a half mile down the road.

My sisters and I were ready for a quiet day, but our little

brother—not quite old enough to join the men—was bored and restless. The sudden stillness was more than he could bear. At midday Mama sent me to investigate what Teddy was up to. I discovered him huddled over a pile of kindling, a sack of marshmallows in one hand and a fistful of kitchen matches in the other. He was obviously preparing for a roast.

"Mama and Daddy have told you a million times not to play with fire!" I screamed.

"It's okay, Sara," he assured me. "I'm making my fire on this sandy spot right under the gas barrels."

I snatched the matches from his hand and marched him to the house where Mama delivered a fierce lecture and a swat across the butt.

It was not enough. A couple of hours later, I found Teddy playing quietly near the strawstack. Using a clipper clothespin, he had invented a device that would strike a match and shoot it high into the air in one swift operation. I was seconds too late. Teddy's latest aim had gone awry, shooting his match into the mantle of straw surrounding the stack. The light flared and raced like a tiny river, winding, licking over the ground. He tried to stamp it out, but the lapping stream was becoming a swift current, tunneling through open channels toward the hot, thirsty center of the stack.

Teddy grabbed a stick and whacked the flames. A plume of dark smoke spiraled upward, warning us that no amount of stamping or pounding would suffice.

I ran for the telephone and rang Central—one short, desperate turn of the crank—yelling *"Fire! Fire at the Hellerud farm!"*

The town siren wailed almost instantly. Soon two red fire engines clanged up the drive, followed by a growling yellow water tanker. Men leaped from the trucks, rolled out their hoses, and aimed them into the inferno. The wind was rising; torrents of water had almost no effect upon the towering flames. The weather vane mounted on the barn roof swirled wildly as the wind shifted to the southwest, gained force and speed, then shifted due south, blowing the burning straw straight toward the barn.

Two firemen tugged on the ropes that hoisted the haymow door, hoping to shield the mow full of dry hay from fiery arrows of straw that sailed on the wind. The men hosed down the barn with great geysers pumped from the tanker, soaking the wooden shingles. Somehow they would have to hold the firebomb below its flash point.

By now Daddy and some members of the threshing crew had joined the firemen. "I don't know if we can get ahead of it with the tankers, Harvey," a fireman said, shaking his helmeted head. "Okay if we start pumping water from your well?"

"Do what you have to," Daddy answered in a shaky voice.

The battle raged all afternoon and into the evening. Mama and Peggy milked the cows inside the threatened barn while Susie and I ran back and forth with sandwiches and Thermoses of coffee for the hungry men, who swallowed them down without even wiping the soot from their hands and faces.

At dusk I noticed a string of cars and pickups lining the gravel road that ran past the farm. A couple of vehicles had even driven into the yard. Their occupants wandered into the denuded oat field; some were milling curiously around the buildings, staring at the strawstack, shielding their eyes against the searing blaze. It was a shocking invasion, more startling than the fire. I saw the fury in Mama's eyes. "Some folks don't have enough to do," is all she said. We were too busy to bother with idle spectators. Gradually they meandered away.

Night fell and still the flames smoldered and flickered back to life. The strawstack shed water like an umbrella, and no amount of dousing could penetrate its burning core. The firemen claimed they had pumped fifteen thousand gallons of water on the stack, and still it burned like a bog of peat. Around midnight a great swiveling crane equipped with a toothed bucket gulped the straw and spewed it out in all directions. A bulldozer finished the job, scattering the soggy remains of Daddy's strawstack far and wide across the scarred pasture.

Teddy watched from an upstairs window, his sisters' arms around him. There was no need to hide—some crimes are too enormous to be punished.

Next morning the cattle surveyed the blackened area in confusion. Hot spots still smoked and flared.

"What will the cows do for bedding when winter comes?" Teddy asked in a small, trembling voice.

"I don't know, Teddy. I just don't know," I answered.

I didn't know, either, that this mountain of amber stems that stood so briefly in the August sunlight would be the last.

It was our final threshing. The next year a modern combine harvested Daddy's crop directly in the field, cutting and threshing the oats all in one efficient operation. A baler came behind to pack and bind the straw for storage under cover in the mow. The crews were disbanded; it was every man for himself. There were no more buckets of potatoes to be peeled, no more lemonade to tote on threshing day. And in a small yet telling way, our world was changed forever.

Dancing the Cows Home

My twin and I were twelve years old when we took up dancing. Inspiration came from an unlikely source: a flamboyant Buick ad in *Look* magazine. The two-page, full-color spread featured a new Roadmaster V-8, contoured like an aircraft, with gleaming grill and bullet taillights. "Power and elegance combined . . . A million dollar ride."

Susie (left) and Sara, dancing on the lawn, 1956

It was not the car that fired our imaginations. It was a pair of ballerinas dressed in crimson feathers, legs split wide, arms extended, sailing over the hood. Those dancers touched our dreams, igniting us with power and grace. We felt gifted, brilliant. We also knew that we would have to work.

We practiced spinning on the lawn, vaulting over milk cans and barbed-wire fences. It was a clumsy beginning, but we persevered all summer, finally noting genuine improvement.

"Toe out!" Susie chided me a dozen times each day, trying to correct my pigeon-toed gait, which posed a serious problem to an aspiring dancer.

Susie thought it might help to watch professional ballerinas on television, then imitate their leaps and turns and gliding grace. With no TV at home, we had to dance three miles down the railroad tracks to Papa Willie's farm. That was our affectionate name for our maternal grandfather, William A. Williamson. We loved to visit him and Grandma Olava. We also loved their new Philco TV and an opportunity to view our favorite shows. We would happily make the trip in hail or sleet if a ballet performance was in store.

Those ethereal dancers, spinning and floating across the stage, provided an irresistible contrast to the workaday world of a Wisconsin dairy farm. Farm women were hopelessly anchored to the soil, outfitted in rough denims, muddy boots, canvas gloves, and paisley bandanas knotted firmly beneath their chins. Susie and I wanted no part of this. We yearned to fly across Swan Lake in filmy gowns and silken slippers.

Never mind that we had no mentor to guide us in our flight. Never mind that we could not flee the farm long or far enough to witness a live ballet performance. Arduous effort and urgent wishing would combine to make our dreams come true.

We studied the magazine and TV ballerinas, then arabesqued across the lawn, believing in our elegance. We pirouetted in the pasture whenever we were sent to fetch the cattle home for evening milking. The dumb animals lumbered along, chewing their cuds, unconcerned that they were driven by two demented butterflies.

As our confidence grew, Susie and I agreed we should begin performing, gaining poise before an audience. Our first stage was the broad, sandy shoulder of the gravel road that formed the western border of our farm. It was not a heavily traveled route, which might be advantageous; the scant traffic would allow us plenty of time to rest and rehearse between acts as we waited for our public to arrive.

The debut was disappointing. Cars and trucks sped quickly by, and their occupants showed no more interest in our antics than had our parents' herd of Holsteins.

Once winter brought the curtain down on our vast outdoor arena, Susie and I created a ballet studio in our upstairs bedroom. We crammed all the furniture into half of the room, then bolted the clothes pole from a spare closet to the opposite wall, forming an exercise bar. We fashioned tights and tutus from starched curtains and long underwear. The result was quite professional.

It was time to dance *en pointe*. We improvised toe shoes from bits of leftover fabric—torturous foot gear, with the round wooden hubs from our brother's set of Tinker Toys and wads of woolen batting stuffed into the toes. We were dedicated to the dance, regardless of the pain and sacrifice.

When we felt ready for the public stage, there was music and choreography to plan. We guessed that Mama might become our pianist without a lot of coaxing. She had confessed to dancing through the cow pasture herself at our age, pretending to be an Egyptian queen. When King Tut's tomb was discovered in 1922, Mama and her younger sister Alice had strutted down the lane, running their oak-branch scepters along the woven wire fences, chanting "King-Tut-*ank*-hamen-nnnn-nnnn-nnnn-nnnn, King-Tut-ank-hamen-nnnn-nnnn-nnnn-nnnn," over and over in 4/4 time. The tightly stretched fence line must have trembled with their song: "King-Tut-*ank*-hamen-nnnn-nnnn-nnnn-nnnn." Their brothers called them "Tut" and "Anky" even now. Susie and I loved this story and asked to hear it again and again. It proved to us that Mama—now so plain and practical—once held some magic in her heart.

Mama scheduled our rehearsals every evening after milking. She helped us choreograph the haunting strains of Schumann's "Traumerei." We foisted our routine on Sunday visitors.

Gradually Susie and I were able to forget our lack of formal training. As prima donnas who had mastered classical ballet through will and energy, we felt compelled to share our art.

In June 1956 when the Milltown Commercial Club sponsored a talent competition open to amateur performers, we were ready to compete. The platform was a wide, flatbed truck parked on Main Street near Miller Hardware and Northwest Electric. It was equipped with a piano and a sound system, blaring three blocks in all directions—the entire length and breadth of Milltown village. This was hardly glamorous staging, but we realized that country ballerinas could not afford to be choosy.

The contest was off to a weary start. There were the usual poor selections we had come to expect at such events. The town librarian gave a fainthearted reading of Robert Frost's "Death of the Hired Man." A high school girl squeaked out an unrecognizable tune on her clarinet. A Lutheran deacon offered up a staid performance of "Swing Low, Sweet Chariot," managing to make the Negro spiritual sound like a German chorale.

Susie and I were next. We were feeling proud and cocky.

The master of ceremonies introduced our act as Susie and I were hoisted aboard the truck. We pranced confidently to center stage. Susie—true to form—stepped up to the microphone and spoke for both of us. My ears burned as I heard the probing questions and Susie's unabashed replies.

"How long have you young ladies been studying ballet?"

"Over a year now, Sir."

"Only a year! And you're dancing in toe shoes already! You must have an excellent teacher."

"Who needs a teacher? Anyway, Mama and Daddy can't afford that, and they don't have the time to take us all the way to

Minneapolis for lessons. So we just teach ourselves."

"That's amazing. How do you do that?"

Susie shrugged. "We just dance. We dance in the haymow and on the railroad tracks and in the cow pasture. At night we dance in our bedroom. Of course Daddy gets pretty mad about all that jumping around up there when he's trying to sleep. One night he came up and belted us. We've learned a lot from watching the dancers on TV—and that's not easy to do when you don't even have a television set!"

Laughter rippled through the audience. A thousand smiling eyes were fixed on us, expecting a hilarious act by clowning stumblebums.

I was furious with my show-off twin whose smart remarks had laid us bare to ridicule. I elbowed Susie in the ribs; she jabbed me

Sara's 1958 attempt at teaching Prissy to dance

back. I wanted to leap from the truck, but there was no escaping till the dance was done.

Mama took her place at the piano and played the opening bars of the Schumann. We lifted off on gusts of faltering faith. Then, like a pair of crippled birds, we knew our stunning handicaps and plummeted to earth. We tried to fly at lower altitudes but tangled and collided on the tiny stage. The final minutes of our dance were limited to timid arabesques and tight little spins that left us nauseous and as weak as the applause.

Susie and I avoided any further mention of the humiliating contest, won by the squeaky clarinet. That night I hid the ballet slippers deep in the closet. My twin never asked me what became of them.

After a couple of days had passed I made a weak attempt at cheering Susie. "What about Priscilla?" I asked brightly.

"What *about* her?"

"Well, I was thinking—maybe we could start teaching her to dance. She's only six. She could get an earlier start than we did. That way she might have a chance . . . "

"No. She doesn't have the build for it. She's too big-boned. And she's pigeon-toed—even worse than you," said Susie crossly.

"She's trainable," I argued, "we really ought to work with her if she shows any interest . . . "

The Hellerud family never did produce a ballerina. But I have proof of the attempt—a photograph of two young girls leaping and twirling on the farmhouse lawn. Their hands are flapping awkwardly, limbs flying in all directions. However, they are toeing out. And smiling broadly.

William Blake once said, "Exuberance is beauty."

If that is true, we were real ballerinas after all.

Weddings

Peggy was a planner who left nothing to chance. In spite of an unshakable religious faith, she knew she must assume an active role in making miracles occur. "God helps those who help themselves," she nagged her carefree younger sisters.

Peggy began working on her most important miracle—her wedding day—in 1953 when she was in the seventh grade at Milltown Junior High. That year Peggy began assembling a scrapbook of sterling silver tableware, crystal goblets, bridal gowns, and diamond solitaires. Her wedding would be the event of the decade—so perfect, so impressive that Milltown society would recall the day in hushed, respectful tones for years to come.

When Peggy turned fifteen and was a sophomore at Milltown High School, she realized the wedding scrapbook was not enough. Time was passing. She must conduct some first-hand research. Susie and I would have to help. Actually she would be helping us, ensuring we were well prepared when our own time came.

At the age of twelve my twin and I had more important things to do than go to weddings, but it wouldn't do to disagree with temperamental Peggy. Besides, she was three years older and wiser and genuinely concerned about our future lives. Half-heartedly we tagged along.

Both Mama and her sister Alice served as organists for local congregations so we were recognized in church and seldom challenged by the ushers. We slipped quietly into the church balcony where we could study the ceremony as unobtrusively as three church mice.

That year we watched a wide variety of weddings—large and small, afternoon and candlelight services, formal, informal, semiformal. They all looked fine to me, but Peggy's critiques were merciless. Wasn't that clinch at the altar just a bit too passionate? It looked as if they couldn't wait. How really tacky, displaying the opened gifts in the church parlor. Not only that—a pregnant bridesmaid! At least the bride looked pure. Peggy explained the meaning of the white wedding gown in a voice choking with emotion.

"It means the bride has saved herself for marriage. She's never let a man go all the way."

"All the way *where?*"

"Don't you get it?" asked Peggy, sounding terribly provoked. "It has to do with babies. Do I have to draw a picture? Do I have to tell you *more?*"

I shook my head. It was obviously a touchy subject. Besides I had a fleeting feeling that the information might be buried somewhere in my dull, distracted mind.

Achieving holy wedlock sounded so precarious. If we were ever going to manage it, my twin and I would have to concentrate.

Our next wedding was an elegant double ceremony, with two sisters vowing to love, honor, and obey their husbands for as long as they all should live. Afterward, my sisters and I explored the possibility of staging a triple ceremony. Feeling coupled for life anyway, Susie and I thought this was a fine idea. Cheaper, too. Peggy selfishly concluded she would not be willing to share the high point of her life with anyone. (By now I realized we were not concerned with happily-ever-after. The wedding was our focus, and the groom was only a prop in the proceedings.) No, she said, Susie and I might as well know that we could count her out of any double deals. When it came to matrimony, she intended to enjoy the starring role. Alone. Susie and I had better pay attention because when it came down to the real thing we would be on our own.

Gradually we assembled a notebook full of wedding tips. More important, we knew all the pitfalls. The wedding of Judy Meyers, a former cheerleader and drum majorette whom we had long envied and admired, was a model of matrimonial disaster.

Poor Judy. Her wedding was a hasty, poorly planned affair; this time we did not wonder why. Yet Judy wore a pure, white wedding gown with scoop neckline, adorned with seed pearls and imported lace. Supported on her father's arm, she lock-stepped up the aisle on a white, satin runner. Her punishment was swift. The organ pedal stuck fast at full volume during the prelude and thundered through the service. The ring bearer dropped both rings at the altar. Two groomsmen searched for several minutes on their hands and knees. The minister coughed and sputtered in midblessing. The best man collapsed without warning, his head striking a basket of sweetheart roses that were strewn across the altar. No sooner was he carried down the aisle than a furious storm descended from the heavens. Lightning struck the steeple, silencing the organ and plunging the congregation into total darkness. Luckily the "I do's" had been uttered just in time. The church was hastily evacuated.

My sisters and I walked home in the soaking rain, pitying poor Judy, the former drum majorette who would strut proudly down Main Street no more.

Peggy thought she had cataloged every possible wedding hazard; she had engineered careful strategies for circumventing every one. But this debacle sent her back to the drawing board. She would insist that every member of her wedding party be examined by a doctor prior to the ceremony. The organ, too, would have to be inspected. No member of the wedding party would be allowed to stand closer than his own body length to flowers or foliage. She would, under no circumstances, consider matrimony in a church that was not thoroughly protected by lightning rods. Really, a bride who overlooked these details was just asking for grief.

We lapsed into silence, quite shaken by the ruinous affair. How could any marriage possibly succeed after such a fiasco? At the very least the newlyweds would have to move away and try to make a new beginning in a far distant place.

Peggy had been right. A wedding did require years of careful planning. Susie and I vowed to take the subject seriously—from this day forward.

The Willie Kids

Taylors Falls Journal
December 1, 1881

A sad accident occurred on the line of the St. Paul and Duluth Railroad near Harris, Minnesota on Tuesday forenoon by which Andrew Williamson (also known as Andreas Wilhelmsen) of Eureka lost his life. He had been to Stillwater and had hired out to work in the pineries this winter. As the train stopped at a station he got off and attempted to board again, falling between the cars in such a manner as to have his arm and leg cut off by the wheels. He lived about five hours after the accident. His remains were brought to this place the same evening.

He leaves a wife and three children in Eureka. The family is in destitute circumstances. A sum of money is being raised in St. Croix Falls to defray his funeral expenses and assist in providing for the family.

My great-grandfather, Andreas Wilhelmsen, emigrated from a meager farm near Bergen, Norway, to northwestern Wisconsin with his wife, Kristi, and three young children in July 1881. Five months later, on his way to a Minnesota logging camp where he hoped to earn some badly needed cash, he fell beneath the wheels of a moving train, severing his left arm and leg. He died five hours later. The family had begun a promising new life in Polk County, Wisconsin, a rolling area with outcroppings of basalt, which recalled the small, rocky farms of their homeland. But, oh, there was such space in this new land! Such fertile soil! Unlimited potential for thriving crops and cattle once the acreage was cleared of rocks and trees. At the time of her husband's death, Kristi was pregnant with a fourth child. Her first news of the accident came with the horse-drawn hearse, delivering the mutilated body.

I heard the story many times as I was growing up. Mama added drama and details through the years.

"Imagine, poor Grandma Kristi having to store his body and those severed limbs in the woodshed until he could be buried in the spring."

"What a courageous woman! She managed four children—one was your Papa Willie—and ran that farm herself for five years, until she married Ole Knutson in 1886."

"When lightning struck the barn the summer of '84, your Grandma Kristi put the fire out herself, carrying buckets of water up a ladder to the hayloft *in her teeth!*"

We accepted even that strange miracle. Such stories came down to us like Gospel. We were the proud and fortunate descendants; we Willie Kids were blessed with some outstanding genes. Straight bones, strong backs. Fine minds. The will to work, achieve, endure.

The evidence lay right before us. Mama's father, Papa Willie, had toppled ninety acres of timber and pulled the stumps like rotten teeth or blasted them out of the ground with dynamite. He had carved a prosperous dairy farm from hardwood forest, managed a cheese factory, helped organize North Valley Lutheran Church, befriended needy neighbors, and raised nine children to adulthood—with no more than a sixth-grade education.

We young people would have the means to go to college.

"You can accomplish anything with such advantages!" Mama exclaimed.

It was something to live up to, this Williamson heritage. Four of Mama's brothers were working their own productive farms near Milltown. Daddy shared machinery as well as haying, threshing, and silo-filling crews with the Williamson brothers. Small and quick and wiry, they seldom stopped to rest; Daddy struggled to match their hard-driving pace. Whenever the hay rope broke, he volunteered to splice it, glad for some quiet minutes to sit alone in the mow and braid the rope. Daddy always made a fine, long splice, a careful work of art. Before it was finished to his satisfaction, a Williamson would holler, "My Gawd, what's taking so long up there, Harvey? We're waiting with another load!"

They worked like demons, even on Sunday. If there was one thing Daddy claimed for himself, it was a restful Sunday afternoon—time to build a birdhouse, write a letter. He might want to motor to his sister's house in Lindstrom, Minnesota. Or simply sit awhile and read the *St. Paul Pioneer Press*.

"Those damned Willies!" Daddy complained. "They treat every day the same. Well, they're not going to make hay at my place on a Sunday. I'll let it take a soaking first."

We kids liked our cheerful, energetic uncles, but they were too busy to pay us much attention. Grandma and Papa Willie had more time for us, and we saw them often, especially after we had moved to Milltown in 1953. In good weather we walked three miles down the railroad tracks, which led straight to their well-kept farm.

By then Papa had turned the big work over to Uncle Wilmar

and a husky hired man. But he did not plan to retire. Papa could usually be found puttering with machinery or doing odd chores in the barn, and he was always delighted to see us.

"Well, I declare!" Then he dug into his chaff-lined pockets and fished out a couple of squashed caramels or sticks of Wrigley's chewing gum. We followed Papa around the barn as he bedded cows and swept the walks, and we begged him to repeat our favorite tales of bygone days.

"Did you really live under the wagon box while you cleared the land and built the log house for Grandma?"

"Tell us how you used to carry home those heavy sacks of flour on your back, all the way from St. Croix Falls."

"Tell us about the time you bought blue patent-leather shoes for Mama and Aunty Alice and the neighbors called you a silly fool for wasting your money and spoiling your little girls that way."

Papa's memories were so sharp and his telling so precise that the stories never varied at all.

Grandma needed coaxing and encouragement. She could usually be found in the house hunched over a basket of knitting or peeling potatoes for the next meal, which was hours away, as if she were still cooking for a crew of threshers. She was small and stooped and permanently tired. Her eyesight was fading, like her recollections, but we knew how to ply her with questions. She rewarded us with distant smiles and sketchy visions of the young Olava Rolstad.

"Look, Grandma, I've drawn this floor plan of the log cabin. Here's the stove and the dining-room table. I've drawn your bed on this end, with a trundle bed beneath, and here's the kids' bed, with three sleeping at the head and two at the foot. Do I have it right?"

"Just about—except the cookstove was over here, with the woodbox in that corner."

"Mama says you taught school at Trap Rock, and that's where you met Grandpa, when you were boarding at his parents' house. That sounds so *romantic*."

"It was nothing but hard work those days. It wasn't romantic at all," Grandma protested, but her eyes were brightening all the same.

Susie and I relished these private times with our grandparents. Their cool, quiet farmhouse with its gabled roof and wide screened porches was a refuge—and a second home.

Once a year we had to share it with fourteen aunts and uncles and twenty-two first cousins at Williamson reunions on the "home place." The gathering was scheduled late in August, between threshing and silo-filling. Even the California aunts—Mugsy and Adele—often managed to travel home for the party.

The buffet table overflowed with potluck casseroles, ham and chicken, sweet corn, Jell-O salads, breads and cakes and pastries, pitchers of hand-squeezed lemonade.

The women chattered in the kitchen, cleaning up after the feast. The men retired to their cribbage boards or smoked their pipes, standing in clusters on the shady lawn. One sweet afternoon each year our uncles smelled of Brylcreem and shaving lotion. They looked fit and trim in crisp shirts and belted slacks rather than the baggy, bibbed overalls that normally hung from their shoulders.

Twenty kids ran in and out, banging the screen doors, taking it all in, unable to relax.

"*Out, kids, out, out, out!* You're bringing in *flies!*" the aunties screamed.

We certainly were. Papa's hip-roofed barn was about sixty yards from the house, and big, black barn flies sailed along with us. They clung to the cakes and casseroles as if they had settled on fresh, fragrant cow pies, yet evaded the fly swatters with lightning speed.

"Stay out, now, please . . ."

We continued to charge in and out and around the house, too excited to sit still and secure in the knowledge that they all loved us anyway. They did think we were wonderful, these collective parents who smiled at the sight of us and let us overhear their praise and bright predictions.

"I tell you, Helen," Aunty Adele would say, "those girls of yours are getting prettier each year. I haven't seen any Hollywood starlets who could match them."

"And such talent, all in one family," Aunty Margaret agreed. "That Peggy is a first-rate scholar."

"Susan will have a brilliant musical career."

"Have you read Sara's latest poems? That girl's less showy than her twin, but I say she's going to surprise us all."

By the time we reached our teens, the Willie Kid identity was stamped on hard with an indelible sense of belonging and high expectations. We attempted some small rebellions, but true as a plumb bob, the weight of Williamson approval swayed us into line. At sixteen I tried smoking cigarettes. Mama saw the Camels in my purse.

"Sara," she said soberly. "What would your grandparents think of that?"

I threw the pack away and never smoked again.

There was no fighting it. I was an upstanding, home-loving Willie Kid. I would have to turn out a respectable weight of work every day as long as I might live.

I was also my father's daughter, imbued with poetry and wanderlust. I sensed that these opposing natures would be warring within me for many years to come.

Grandma Launsby

At the age of twelve, my twin and I were not looking for another grandma. We had three grandparents already and plenty of other relatives living all around us in the 1950s. Looking or not, we found her—an honorary grandma who widened our horizons and brought depth and drama to our lives.

We did not call her Grandma right away, for she was a large, imposing woman with angular features and a high, shrill voice. Furthermore, she claimed connections to the Danish royal family. The Countess Ebba Trampe Westergaard Launsby, once a coloratura soprano, accomplished pianist, and composer, lived in an unlikely place: Luck, Wisconsin. Apparently her noble birth and fine education had failed to shield her from a series of misfortunes. Once divorced and twice widowed, the countess was living an isolated, lonely existence when our mother first knocked on her door on a June evening in 1955.

By now Susie had devoted five years of intensive study to the piano. She had devoured the Schaum piano books and completed the John Thompson series, hungering for more. "I really can't offer Susan what she needs now," admitted the teacher, a neighbor from Balsam Lake who had coached my twin since she was seven. "Already she can outperform me. She has strong hands, nimble fingers, and an unusually good ear. I've never seen such motivation in a child so young. Is there any way you folks could get her into Minneapolis for weekly lessons?"

That would have meant four precious hours lost from every Saturday, which seemed impossible, at least until Teddy was old enough to help substantially with farming chores.

Soon after that Mama learned that a Danish countess—said to be reclusive and eccentric but a highly skilled musician—was living in Luck, only eight miles north of Milltown. Mama paid the countess a visit and asked if she might accept Susie as a piano student. The countess declared that she had little interest in working with children—particularly a young person of Norwegian descent. But she reluctantly agreed to grant Susie an audition in her home the following week.

That was a glad event. Susie found her mentor; the countess gained new energy and purpose in this ambitious, gifted child who had sprung like a miracle from the cow pastures and cornfields of Polk County.

Susie returned home from her Wednesday evening piano lesson wide-eyed with excitement. She kept me awake past midnight describing this aristocratic woman and her elegant two-story home. The house itself, said Susie, was not unlike our own, but the interior was festooned with rose-colored draperies, ancient faded tapestries, oil paintings of European nobles, and life-size family portraits hung in ornate frames. German, French, and Danish books of art and history lined one parlor wall from floor to ceiling, lending the house an air of ancient knowledge.

The countess owned a jeweled crown called a "tiara," which she stored in a secret compartment of her desk. One drawer contained a brass stamp bearing the family coat of arms and a bar of red-brown sealing wax. The countess had demonstrated these utensils, striking a kitchen match, melting a thick pool of wax upon the flap of a parchment envelope, then stamping and sealing her official letter to the Danish embassy.

A white angora cat presided over the impressive ritual. This aloof, high-stepping creature seemed to understand that he belonged to a royal household.

I had to see for myself. The following Wednesday evening I tagged along to Susie's lesson. Everything was true. A high-born person did indeed reside in the village of Luck. And if further proof were needed, tacked to a wall in the rear hallway was a huge poster with a photograph of the countess in her younger days. She proudly translated the bold, black Danish words:

Renowned Pianist and Coloratura Soprano
Ebba Trampe
Of the Danish Royal Conservatory, Copenhagen, Denmark
In Concert—June 15, 1929

The countess had been a beautiful young woman. The years had faded her blue eyes and thinned her graying hair, which she piled carelessly atop her head and anchored with jeweled combs. She moved her heavy body slowly, bracing her arthritic spine with large splayed hands. Her head was high, her chin thrust forward, feet set wide. At sixty-five, the countess retained a powerful, if less than graceful, presence.

I sat reverently on the pink, brocade sofa while Susie and her mentor labored at the piano. The countess was no longer a skilled performer. Her stiffened fingers stumbled over the keyboard, but she compensated for her lost ability with fierce encouragement and stinging observations.

"I wouldn't give ten cents for your training, Darling! In fact, whoever taught you these bad habits should be flogged. But you have a *marvelous* talent! Now let us proceed!" She praised Susie's coordination, her lively sense of rhythm, and her keen ear for color and shading.

The piano was a Baldwin Acrosonic with a stiff action, slightly out of tune. The countess admitted that she missed her fine, old Steinway back in Copenhagen. "But then, one must always make the best of whatever is available. If we wait for perfect timing and ideal conditions, we will accomplish nothing."

When the lesson was over, she warmly invited me to return with Susie the following Wednesday evening; the angora cat had been rubbing against my ankles all evening. "I trust his instincts.

Susie and Grandma Launsby, 1955

He is an excellent judge of character. You will always be welcome in my house."

Before another month had passed, the countess had become our "Grandma Launsby" and we were her own dear "Sweetie-pies."

We walked the mile into Milltown and took the afternoon train to Luck, arriving early so we could mow her lawn and run her various errands in the village. Grandma treated us to imported Danish sardines and liver pâté and fruit soups and taught us how to handle finger bowls and linen serviettes—her fancy name for napkins.

"As a renowned musician, Susan, you will be an honored guest in fine society one day. You will visit the grandest homes and concert halls in Europe. Sara will be your companion. I must see that you are both prepared."

Mama seemed pleased about the social tutoring, since she had little time to correct our careless manners. We were allowed to hop the train and visit Grandma Launsby whenever we wished. By now the cat was greeting us with cool indifference. We guessed he must feel jealous that his mistress lavished her attention on two interlopers—attention that had once been his alone.

Eventually the music lessons extended to overnight visits. Before bedtime Grandma entertained us with fascinating stories of her youth—her unhappy marriage to a Swedish nobleman and early married life in Russia, their penniless escape during the Bolshevik Revolution, her divorce and flight back to Denmark, to Germany, and finally to America. Then we bedded down under silken comforters, surrounded by antique books and paintings. We slept like pampered princesses, dreaming of adventure and romance that waited at the distant corners of the world.

It puzzled us that everyone in Milltown seemed so ordinary, while Grandma's life—only four miles down the track—was filled with saints and villains. She was quick to judge everyone she met as totally virtuous, utterly evil, or—worse than that—hopelessly stupid. She could render heartless but hilarious impersonations of those who fell into the latter category. Many of these imbeciles, it seemed, were the good-hearted common folks of Luck, Wisconsin. Grandma liked to stomp around the parlor warbling a modern hymn, "How Great Thou Art," fortissimo. She purposely hit the high notes a quarter tone off pitch, imitating Mrs. Chase, wife of the local cheesemaker and self-appointed leader of the church choir.

"She thinks she's so grand!" sputtered Grandma when she could get her breath. "Everywhere I go I have to suffer farmers and peasants who have the brains and manners of a chicken!"

Grandma must have seen Susie and me exchanging doubtful glances, for she was quick to exclaim, "Not you, my darlings! You have beauty and intelligence. You will go far in this world, and I can teach you everything you need to know."

She coached us in the rules of fine deportment.

"Always, always keep your spine straight, chin forward. And smile in company, even when you feel like crying."

"Curtsy deeply, with your right foot forward, left leg back. Bend straight from the waist . . . face up, *smiling* . . . "

"Hold your hands still. No fidgeting or nail-biting."

"Chewing gum is common; never let me see you use it."

"Never share yourselves too cheaply. And never, never allow a boy to kiss you until he has promised marriage."

Most of the advice was reasonable, except for that final counsel, which we guessed might pose some problems in the future. We vowed to hold to a higher standard.

We wondered privately whether such high-class etiquette would leave us as friendless as Grandma Launsby seemed to be. Fancy manners might look "uppity" to our rural Wisconsin neighbors.

Susie reminded me that we did not plan to stay in Polk County a day beyond our high school graduation. Besides, Grandma was rejected for more complicated reasons. She had given us a sketchy background, describing her second marriage to a Danish-American named Frede Westergaard, whose grown children had "persecuted" her throughout her dismal years in Nebraska. When Frede died, he had left his unhappy widow a family home in the village of Luck, Wisconsin, and she had moved there, far from the mean step-children.

A third marriage, to Hans Launsby, had been equally disastrous. Hans, who sold farm produce in a leaking timber shed adjacent to the Luck feed mill, had expected his aristocratic wife to handle unwashed eggs, muddy vegetables, and rotting fruit. She had been rude and haughty to his customers and later found it was impossible to make amends. Worse than that, poor Hans soon bored her to distraction. She had actually felt relieved when he became ill and "passed on to glory."

Grandma never explained why she elected to remain in Luck, and we thought it might be brazen to inquire. Perhaps it was a lack of funds. We supposed that even a countess might be suffering financial woes. And she had hinted of some quarrels with royal relatives. Even her daughter in Copenhagen wrote only once a year, a terse greeting penned on the back of a small Christmas card.

Staying in Luck was not a happy choice for Ebba Launsby. The townspeople eyed her with suspicion; a few were openly hostile as she went about her business on Main Street. "Good morning *your highness* . . . Do we have anything grand enough for you today?"

Grandma reacted by making imperious demands as she felt befit her station. Susie and I began doing much of her shopping in order to spare Grandma Launsby—and the merchants—these trying encounters.

We offered to buy a can opener on our next trip to the hardware store, finding no such device in her cluttered kitchen. Grandma wouldn't have it.

"All that's needed," she said, "is a hammer and a butcher knife. A Russian soldier taught me this useful trick some forty years ago."

Eager to demonstrate, she seized one weapon in each hand. She pounded and sliced her way into the can, winding up with only half the tuna left inside a wickedly sharp six-pointed metal star. The cat leaped about her feet as he cleaned up the spillage. At this point the newsboy appeared at the door for his weekly collection. The sight of an agitated old woman behind the screen, brandishing a butcher knife in one hand and a hammer in the other, sent the lad running for his life. After this ill-timed episode, Grandma had terrible trouble getting anything delivered to her door.

Grandma further destroyed her image one Sunday morning when she thought she spied her neighbor receiving from—rather than giving to—the church collection plate. She popped up from her pew, shrieking, "Thief, thief!" No one responded.

"Blessed be the tie that binds . . . Our hearts in Christian love . . . " The postlude was subdued. So was Grandma's reception in the foyer. No one shook her hand or thanked her for her Christian intervention. She was no longer welcome in the Danish Lutheran Church.

No, an eccentric high-born lady like Ebba Launsby did not mix well in this humble society of farmers and shopkeepers. Susie and I knew we had begun to fill a void in her lonely life. What we had embarked upon as carefree love took on the weight of duty and responsibility. We were already schooled in that, and we tried hard to meet her needs.

Now and then Grandma attempted to find my "God-given talent." It confounded her that Susie's identical twin sister exhibited no special aptitudes, and she yearned to correct the deficiency.

But her best efforts to make me an opera diva met with failure. "Your voice is so tiny," Grandma sighed. "Project, project, *project!*"

After the voice lessons stopped, she concentrated on my literary leanings. She could translate my poetry and prose into five languages; her high connections with European publishers guaranteed my international success. Eager to please, I produced an essay on soil conservation and another on the evils of the labor unions.

"That's fine," said Grandma. "But I'm not sure we can find a publisher. Why don't you try writing a poem about something—or someone—very close to your heart?"

That was a simple assignment, and the results won me high praise from my mentor.

To Susie

I love her more than summer
  with all its fragrant flowers.
I love her more than springtime
  with its singing birds and showers.
I love her more than autumn
  with its leaves of red and gold.
I love her more than winter
  with its snowy blanket cold.
I love her more than oceans deep
  and more than skies of blue
Yes, I love my sister Susie
  and I know she loves me too.

Grandma Launsby translated the verse into Danish and submitted it to a Copenhagen newspaper where she claimed it was printed. But she was never able to produce a copy for me, and I suspected she was only trying to spare my feelings.

I began doing more and more yard work, household chores,

and errands while Grandma coached my talented twin. I felt both dejected and relieved.

"I love you equally!" she often said, as if denying a painful, private truth. "The music is just something extra. . . . You're both my granddaughters . . . you always will be."

Like a true relative, Grandma Launsby could embarrass us beyond belief. Accompanying her to church could be mortifying, even when she kept her mind off the collection plate. Her powerful operatic soprano soared high above the congregation, causing all eyes to turn in our direction. Attending a musical event with her was worse.

"Listen, Susan!" she would hiss loudly, unconcerned that the performer's relatives were seated all around. "No expression! No feeling! Beethoven must be spinning in his grave!"

During our thirteenth winter, Susie and I joined Grandma for a shopping expedition in the city. We boarded the train with her in Luck and disembarked in Minneapolis. When she was unable to summon a taxicab at the depot, Grandma approached private drivers who were climbing into their cars, demanding that they deliver us to Dayton's Department Store. She was coldly ignored. She stepped into traffic then, shaking her fist and threatening all who failed to comply. Susie and I retreated, gazing skyward, pretending not to know this shrill, obnoxious woman. Finally we hailed a cab ourselves, calmed Grandma, and were safely on our way.

Grandma had no driver's license and carried no personal identification. She had no need for that in Luck, Wisconsin. When the clerk in Dayton's shoe department refused to cash her check, Grandma felt abused and insulted. Her excited voice could be heard past many racks of shoes, through Better Dresses and beyond.

"I am the Countess Ebba Trampe Westergaard Launsby of the Danish royal family! No one has ever questioned it before!" She flashed the emeralds and amethysts that adorned her fingers, tore the ruby broach from her coat lapel, and dug in her handbag for family photographs and monogrammed handkerchiefs.

A crowd began to gather. The flustered sales clerk hurried away to consult her superior. At last a dignified gentleman appeared, assuring Grandma she could put away her jewels. She was so obviously a regal woman. The sales clerk simply had not been prepared for such distinguished clientele.

"I beg your pardon, Madam," he concluded. "Your check will be accepted without further delay."

Shortly before our fifteenth birthday, Grandma Launsby confided to Susie and me that she was ill with cancer. We had known about her mastectomy, for when she pressed us close we felt a full bosom on her left side and almost a cavern on her right. There was a large prosthesis hanging on the back of her bedroom door, which Grandma wore only on rare occasions when she dressed up to meet the "real" world beyond the village of Luck. But we had known her three years now, and the surgery had taken place some time before that. We had not worried much about it.

Now she told us that the cancer was ravaging her bones. She would return to Denmark where the government would pay for her expensive care. She would forgive longstanding family grievances in order to be buried with counts and kings.

Mama, Susie, and I helped Grandma with a public sale of her household goods. It was a sunny day—July 12, 1958. The curious villagers turned out in force. They rummaged through Grandma's fine furnishings and housewares, which we had neatly displayed on chairs and tables all across the lawn. Brocade draperies, tapestries, silverware, fine china, books, and paintings were quickly auctioned, snatched up, and toted off by strangers. That evening Grandma presented us with gifts that she had salvaged from the auction—lace handkerchiefs, silver goblets, rings, and pendants. I pretended not to notice that the finest gifts went to my favored twin. Susie was also entrusted with an oil painting of a royal mother and her infant daughter. The young Ebba in the portrait wore an angelic smile; the jeweled tiara rested like a halo in her soft brown hair.

I felt genuine loss. I was also secretly consoled that this complicated, needy woman would soon disappear. Maybe now I would lose a troubling sense of a growing distance from my twin.

Grandma Launsby would be leaving the next morning on the outbound train. We agreed farewells were wrenching and promised not to come and wave good-bye. Grandma knew she would be meeting us in heaven. She also knew that God would furnish a piano. With any luck it would be a Steinway grand.

December 8, 1955
Dear Adele and Mugsy,

I'm writing this to both of you because you share your mail anyway and I'm sure a poke at writing. The twins wrote the enclosed letters a week ago to tell you about their trip to Minneapolis during Thanksgiving vacation and I held them, hoping to add a letter.

The twins went to Minneapolis by train with Mrs. Launsby Thanksgiving afternoon after having dinner here. Mrs. Launsby had scheduled a number of "engagements" for them through a Danish friend named Brita Armstrong whom I gather has both money and influence to spare. I went down on Saturday AM by bus, arriving in time for Mrs. Armstrong's tea, and we all came home by bus together Saturday night.

The kids had a glorious time and looked very, very nice in their nylon dresses and ruffled petticoats. I had to shorten the waists only an inch and the skirts about 3 inches. The petticoats were okay for length now, so you see they have grown since our summer shopping spree. I don't think we could have chosen a better style. The sleeves are butterfly cut so no shoulders to get outgrown and I think they'll get 2 seasons wear out of them at least. (I left the inch on the waist underneath and have a generous hem.) Needless to say I was proud of them at the tea party. The friends of Mrs. Armstrong were duly impressed with their ability, but nicest of all is the fact that they are very modest and unspoiled. They put on no frills or airs and seemed so comfortable among those fine-feathered women that I was just amazed. To tell the truth I didn't feel uncomfortable either and came away with the feeling that I am richer by far than most of them and I envy them not one bit of their fine Persian rugs and Cadillacs. It was a nice experience and one the kids will never forget. Eugenie Andersen, the Danish ambassador and guest of honor, could not be present after all. But the girls did the little ballet to Eugenie Andersen's Waltz and that was the cutest of all.

Mrs. Ridenauer, the lady whose house they slept at and who arranged the TV and radio appearances, lives in an old mansion out on Pleasant Avenue. I didn't get to see her house but the kids say she has furniture from an old plantation and 20 Persian rugs. She and her family are from the south originally and she speaks with quite an accent. Her husband is a heavy drinker and Mrs. Launsby says they really can't afford to stay on in that big place under the circumstances. Mrs. R. wanted to keep Susan and Sara over Sunday in hopes of getting a recording made of one of Susan's piano compositions for a fellow who she says is President of First National Banks and has some connection with getting scholarships for young musicians.

Mrs. Launsby was not in favor of staying over and since I couldn't, we all came home together. Mrs. Launsby is a little possessive where Susan is concerned and at first I thought she resented anyone else's interest in her, but I think she really has Susan's welfare at heart. She said nothing would come of it anyway and it would be added expense. Better to wait until Susan is a few years older and has more experience before going after such things. She has much to learn and can do that right here taking lessons while she goes to school.

We heard the two minute program on radio with Jimmy Valentine (KSTP) but missed the performance on T.V. It was 20 below here that day and we thawed water pipes until 3 PM. Mama saw it quite by accident. I surely wish I had known when it would be showing and I'd have left the frozen pipes and gotten myself over to the home farm somehow to watch it. Harvey said, "Oh, well—we hear Susan playing Chopin every day, and Sara will read that poem any time we ask her," but of course he's sorry that he missed it too.

I'll try to send some pictures with my next letter.

Hope all is well with you and yours—

Love,

Helen

Buying on Time

When I study Mama's neat household ledgers from the 1950s, I realize that in a few short decades the world of everyday commerce has been turned completely upside down. While we commonly buy groceries with cash these days, nearly everything else is purchased with plastic, readily available "on time." We are so confident of our future prosperity, so willing to mortgage our tomorrows.

It wasn't always so.

Mama bought her sugar, flour, tea, and oatmeal from the Milltown Co-op at the east end of Main Street. She bought thread and buttons, cards of rick-rack, socks, underwear, and mousetraps there as well. The Co-op was housed in a long, low timber structure, with a hammered tin ceiling and creaking wooden floors. Packaged groceries, meat, and produce were stocked at one end, dry goods on the other. Dry goods, I reasoned, must be anything not edible, ranging from work boots to baby bonnets. Regular customers bought staples and minor household supplies on credit and settled their accounts about the tenth of each month, as soon as the milk check arrived from Stella Cheese.

Mama shopped there every other Saturday. As she stashed away her new supplies, she folded and flattened the brown wrapping paper and carefully wound all the store string into one great ball, bristling with knots. She scrutinized the cash-register tape, checking off each purchase as she placed it in a cabinet or on the pantry shelf. Mama circled any errors—including those in her favor—and set the tape aside to be rectified on her next trip to town.

Except for the convenient monthly tab at the Co-op, a smart farmer did not buy without the cash in hand. This applied even to such major purchases as farm implements or vehicles. And where the family auto was concerned it was wise to maintain a modest image. Daddy understood this well. When he decided to get a paint job on his eight-year-old Kaiser, bought in 1951 for five hundred dollars, he chose the same pale shade of blue, although he had never liked the color. It would not do to have the neighbors think he bought another car when what he really needed was a bigger silo or new shingles on the barn.

It was simple, really. There were only three commandments, chiseled in the stone of prudent living, carefully handed down from parent to child:

1. Never live beyond your means
2. Pay cash
3. Support your local merchants.

Helen and Harvey Hellerud, 1955

There were a few minor exceptions. The Sears Roebuck catalog was all right for goods that were not locally available. A woman had to rely on the mail-order catalog even more if she lived far from town and had small children to mind at home. She might also buy a whisk broom from the Fuller Brush man or a bottle of vitamins from the Watkins dealer when one of them came to call. The shopper might be eager for adult conversation. She could make a modest purchase now and then, guaranteeing his return visits without doing serious damage to the local economy.

No one could criticize that. But there were always a few high-hatted folks who had to test the rules. They were mostly townspeople who went to Dayton's or Donaldson's Department Stores in Minneapolis to look for fashions or home furnishings that would set them apart from their country neighbors. It was rumored that several families even bought on time. Mama wondered aloud how any woman could enjoy the coat on her back when it belonged to a department store or lending institution. These finely dressed folks were often the same ones who dropped a thin dime into the church collection plate. Mama declared that such greed, such poor management, was worse than "being on the dole." And if they didn't mend their ways, that was exactly where these spendthrifts could expect to be.

Except for the mortgage on the farm, Mama and Daddy never bought a single thing on time. It was a matter of both pride and practicality. Farmers could not afford to gamble with their land, their very livelihood, for mere vanities. No matter how hard a farmer worked, he could not plan on prosperity. Uncertain markets, unlucky weather, a barn full of ailing cattle, or a plague of army worms could eat up all his profits in a single season. No, we would never see our parents betting on the corn crop or mortgaging their future checks from Stella Cheese.

So we were all astonished on the day that Mama and Daddy broke their own rules of sound economy. All three commandments were shattered in one mighty stroke. This could only happen for the most compelling need, the most exalted purpose. In 1956 this could happen only for a piano.

On the eighteenth day of June a piano salesman drove into our yard with a beautiful Baldwin spinet loaded in the back of his truck. He had come seventy miles from Minneapolis. We never asked who sent him or how he knew about Susie's ambition to become a concert pianist. Perhaps someone had tipped him off, describing our old upright piano with its dark, bubbling varnish, chipped ivories, worn-out hammers, and broken strings.

Whatever—or whoever—led this salesman to us, his timing was perfect. It was a sunny day; the tender crops were thriving. The piano was perfect, too. It was slim and low and blonde—a Baldwin Acrosonic, with an even action and a bright, clear sound. Susie hopped up inside the truck and began playing Chopin mazurkas on the spinet, closing her eyes and leaning into the music as if she were performing in a concert hall. The music rang off the side panels, bounced off the floor and ceiling, and funneled out the tailgate where Mama stood deep in conversation with the piano man. He was aiming at her highest hopes, her sweetest dreams. Mama proudly gave him a tour of the house and pointed out her children's artwork and poetry that adorned the walls.

"Such remarkable young people!" he exclaimed. "I can see that your children have superior intelligence and creativity. I could tell you their I.Q.'s without knowing any more."

"Well, actually, they've all done exceptionally well in school."

"This is obviously a family of culture. And I would venture, Ma'am, that you are musical yourself."

"Well, yes, I used to play both piano and violin, but now it's hard to find the time . . . "

"I'm sure it is."

"I played the violin for several years with a local chamber group. We practiced evenings in one another's homes. It got pretty late sometimes. My kids used to sneak out of bed and listen in the stairwell."

"No doubt all that fine music influenced your daughter," the salesman said, nodding toward the concert still flowing from the truck.

"Well, we concentrated on the classics—Mozart, Bach, Beethoven. And we had some talented musicians."

Probably the salesman had learned enough about our mother's string quartet. He side-stepped toward the truck and cupped his ear to hear the young musician better who could help him close this sale.

"Just listen to her! Such technique, such sensitive interpretation!"

Rachmaninoff crashed off the metal walls, rolled from the tight, harsh space.

Daddy drove up on his noisy John Deere, mopped his face with a greasy red bandanna, swung down from the tractor seat, and joined the conference. The salesman did not lose a beat.

"What an amazing child!" he exclaimed. "Only thirteen years old? One day she will be performing on the great stages of the world. I have to move her out of there."

He dropped the loading gate. Susie stood aside while he dollied the piano down from the truck onto the soft grass. Susie slipped back onto the bench and continued to make music for any of God's creatures blessed with ears to take it in. She was playing a Bach prelude now, with shoots of green corn at her back and lambs dancing in the pasture nearby.

Daddy stepped aside, rubbing the back of his neck, a gesture of confusion. Mama approached him cautiously.

"I didn't order it, Harvey, really. . . . Maybe Susan's piano teacher had something to do with this."

The salesman moved deftly between them. "She must have this instrument," he declared. He dabbed his eyes with a fresh, white handkerchief.

Of course she must. If Daddy had a single doubt, he never voiced it. The price tag was $1,099, a minor matter that no one discussed until the piano was positioned in the living room. The massive old upright was carted out. With some difficulty, Daddy and the salesman loaded it into the truck. The salesman offered to haul it away at no extra charge.

There was a small matter of some paperwork, a contract to be signed, interest to be calculated over the thirty-month installment period. Mama scrubbed off the oilcloth on the kitchen table. She served tea and oatmeal cookies while Daddy double-checked the figures. All five kids stood in the doorway, watching in amazement as our parents signed away a portion of their monthly income to the Wylie Music Company. The salesman said he would be mailing a booklet of payment coupons for their convenience. Every month they should remit one coupon with a check for $22.40, beginning on the first day of August.

We never imagined that a musical instrument could cost so much. We would not be able to talk about this at church or school, either. That would not fit with Daddy's rules regarding modesty and private family business. Besides, people would say we were crazy. Or lying. Or both.

Just to make sure we weren't dreaming, we ran into the living room where the spinet beamed like a patch of sunshine.

"It isn't just for me," Susie began awkwardly. "Whenever any of you wants to play, just push me off the bench. This piano belongs to the whole family."

"Okay," we all agreed.

Teddy and Priscilla crossed the room and began a reverent tinkling in the upper octaves. Susie, Peggy, and I stood rooted in the doorway.

I knew I was never going to play that piano. I was not going to compete with Susie for the spotlight. I would have to find some other way to shine.

The installment piano was a family windfall all the same. It was a reckless, brilliant gamble. It was a pledge to healthy cattle, ample rainfall, sunny skies—tomorrow.

Arlie

Close timing never surprised us. As identical twins Susie and I expected to cross every threshold together. Our tandem leap into adolescence was no exception. Within two days of each other—in August 1956—we needed the Kotex belts and pads stored in our bottom bureau drawer. We shopped together at the Milltown Co-op, selecting Munsingwear training bras with a single pink rosebud blooming between the flat cotton cups. We had no breasts to train as yet but knew our bodies would be changing soon, reshaping and expanding rapidly. We felt a troubling loss of self-control.

That year we both started keeping journals, as well as long, compulsive lists of everything from daily tasks to lifelong goals. The journals gave us a place to express what we could not say even to each other. The record keeping helped to anchor our heaving lives.

Susie assigned herself a list of weekly chores and lined them out as she accomplished them: (1) Mow lawn, (2) Clean house, (3) Write to pen pal, (4) Practice piano 4 hours/day, (5) Memorize Bach Prelude.

I inventoried our wardrobe and maintained a shopping list: (1) Pop-beads, (2) White flats, (3) Roll-sleeve blouse, (4) Black Ban-lon sweater, (5) Poodle skirt. I seldom acquired any of these items but found it comforting to catalog my needs. I crossed the items off as they faded from fashion and replaced them with my latest longings.

Acrobats, 1955, Sara in the supporting role

I also listed five or six young men who occupied my fantasies. Their ranking shifted often. The list gave me a satisfying surge of power. Heroes rose and fell according to my daily whims, and I awarded extra points for smiles aimed in my direction. I expected nothing more; most of my "boyfriends" were distant idols—high school athletes who scarcely knew my name.

Susie thought this list was silly, but she shared an interest in one of my choices. His name was Arlie Anderson, and he knew our names well enough, although he never seemed able to tell us apart. He was the hired man on Papa Willie's farm, an eager worker, best that Papa had ever had. Arlie was eighteen, tall and slim with wavy hair and soft brown eyes. He might have topped my list except for crooked, decaying teeth that marred his easy smile.

Susie and I made frequent trips to our grandparents' farm that summer, hiking three miles down the railroad tracks and arriving early in the evening to help Arlie with chores in the barn. We poured heavy buckets of warm milk into the strainers, fed calves, scraped and limed the walks, anything we could do to hurry him along. Finally Arlie strode toward the house and into the washroom off the back porch. We heard him scrub his hands and arms, his face and neck with a gritty, green bar of Lava soap. He always took the time to change his shirt so that he smelled flower fresh when he joined us in the parlor.

Both Grandma and Papa were losing their eyesight, and we could count on having the television to ourselves. Arlie settled into the broad upholstered chair. Susie and I perched primly on either side. Gradually his long arms slid around our waists and drew us down into his lap. There was little need for conversation. We were fully focused on Arlie's tight-muscled thighs, only half aware of the parade of programs marching noisily across the screen: *Alfred Hitchcock* . . . *Ed Sullivan Show* . . . *What's My Line?* . . . *This Is Your Life* . . . *You Asked for It* . . . The cathode vapors wrapped all three of us in humid closeness and beamed us to a dusky blue heaven. We hovered there, transfixed for hours until Mama came—always too soon—to fetch us home.

Later that summer Grandma had her cataracts removed. She would be needing help around the house for several days. Susie was busy preparing for a piano competition, and I agreed to go alone. Mama said I'd best stay overnight. The men would want their breakfast early—pancakes, eggs, and sausages at 6 A.M.

I ran down the railroad tracks in a cold, gray rain, arriving hot and sticky, drenched with nervous perspiration. It would be entirely different sitting alone with Arlie in the parlor, curled like a kitten in his lap. At last I would not have to share. I would try to talk, of course, but my throat would close up tight—my words would suffocate with love. My heart would thump inside my chest. Arlie would finally know, and he would gasp that he adored me, too. Tears would stream down both our faces.

"What are we going to do? I'm so awfully young . . . "

"I will wait—wait until you are eighteen if I have to. I must have you for my wife."

"What about Susie?"

"She'll get over it. She has her piano. Anyway, it can't be helped—it's you I love."

Reality was a cruel departure from this fantasy. Arlie cleaned up after chores as usual, changing even his pants and shoes, then spun out of the driveway in his blue-and-white Impala. He was gone for hours.

I was lying wide awake on the parlor sofa when the white shafts of his headlights pierced the room and slid across the wall above my head. I fanned my long straight hair over the pillow, closed my eyes, and practiced breathing slowly, deeply. I heard the back door open, close, and latch. I heard his footsteps approach, stop at the open parlor door. Enter. I sensed him standing over me, close enough to feel my quivering breath. He sat, then, on the edge of the sofa, and the smell of beer and stale tobacco washed against my face.

"Susie!" he whispered urgently, shaking my shoulder. My jaw locked tight. My body froze.

"Sara?" he tried again, and I was liquified, reaching out with eager arms.

He kissed me then, over and over, with deep, wet sounds, and I was sucked into a cavernous mouth, all lips and tongue and beery breath, no teeth to anchor me, to save me from an utter drowning. I clung to him and let him swallow me.

He belched. "I think I'm sick . . . " And he was gone.

I heard him retching in the bathroom overhead.

Dawn was a long time coming, and I didn't sleep at all. I didn't think about Arlie. I thought about Susie, how strangely separate I felt from her. I thought about being thirteen, with a woman's hips and itchy, swollen nipples, still waiting for my breasts.

Arlie came to the breakfast table looking cross and pale. He was careful not to look my way; he did not speak or smile. He sipped some coffee and rudely shoved his scrambled eggs aside.

"Don't feel bad, Honey," Papa whispered after Arlie had left the room. "It's not your cooking. Poor kid had all those rotten teeth pulled out, you know. He'll get his dentures in a week or two—that should improve his appetite."

I watched him shuffle toward the barn, a loutish young farmhand wearing baggy denims and a seed corn cap. I wanted desperately to hurry home and list this somewhere; when the pen was finally in my hand I didn't know what list to turn to or what words to write.

Charming Company

Following the move to Milltown in 1953, our parents transferred their church membership from Faith Lutheran to Milltown Evangelical Lutheran Church. In 1957 Daddy was elected deacon, and Mama commandeered the choir. We kids were Sunday-schooled and catechized, confirmed as Lutherans. At fourteen, Susie began serving as church organist. Peggy and I offered our alto voices every Sunday, trying to help balance Mama's choir. We struggled to hold our own against six mature sopranos, who competed with each other in piercing vibrato.

Nearer my God to Thee,
Nearer to Thee!

E'en though it be a cross
That raiseth me . . .

We had barely finished the processional, and already I was feeling restless. I could not see how all this church-going was bringing me nearer to God, since I was pretty sure that He hung out in forests, ponds, and pasturelands rather than this stuffy church balcony.

Possibly my parents would agree, but we had never discussed it. Religion was a highly private matter in our household. We never uttered grace at the table, critiqued the Sunday sermon, or held family prayers or Bible readings. Surely clean living was the ticket to the Heavenly Kingdom, if such a place existed. And if it did, Mama and Daddy would be the first enrolled. Peggy's name must be high on that list as well. As a young child she had prayed enough to cover a lifetime of sinning. Lately she seemed to be losing fervor and finding a better sense of balance. Thank God, I thought, because this whole religion business could really get quite out of hand if you were not careful.

I did not worry much about my parents going overboard. Their expanding church involvement appeared to have a social basis. As Mama said, "We can't afford to live our lives in isolation. A person has to give some time and talent back to the community."

Mama and Daddy had never been short on talent, and now, with a more efficient farm, they found a few spare hours to give. Gradually they took on added obligations at Milltown Evangelical Lutheran. Mama joined the Ladies Aid and baked cakes, bars, and casseroles for the church suppers. Daddy met with the building committee, laying plans for a parish hall adjacent to the church.

While praying remained a private matter, church finances and politics were openly discussed at home. Mama and Daddy took pride in a giving spirit. They pledged generously to the building fund, even though our sheep shed was leaking and the kitchen linoleum was cracked and worn, in desperate need of replacement. Mama seemed both proud and irritated. "We won't be replacing the kitchen floor this year—not after making that hundred-dollar pledge for the parish hall."

"Your father puts a paper dollar in the collection plate every Sunday," she reminded us often. "I see some town folks who should have money to spare, dropping in nothing but small change."

Daddy feigned a grudging attitude. "Forty thousand dollars!" he exploded as we drove home from church in the second-hand De Soto, which he had reluctantly purchased after the total breakdown of his '46 Kaiser. "I could buy three good farms for that! How can a damn parish hall cost forty thousand dollars when you can buy a hundred acres of good farmland for ten?"

I knew he was pleased about his increased involvement in church affairs. And he was exaggerating some. We had bought the Milltown farm for twelve thousand dollars in 1953. The outbuildings had been neglected, the soil depleted. Four years later with improvements, fertilizing, crop rotation, and escalating values, the land was worth nearly twice what we had paid for it. Mama liked to remind Daddy of that happy fact.

"Sure, it would be worth twenty or more if I could find some poor fool willing to buy it!" he exclaimed. "Who would want to pay that kind of money for the privilege of working like a fool slave for the rest of his life?"

Mama would not answer. We all knew how she loved dairying. And Daddy seemed pretty well reconciled to it, now that they were finally making progress. He did enjoy the field work. He could ride around on the John Deere towing a combine or a cultivator for hours in the dusty heat and come home whistling at sundown. Our parents claimed we five kids were their "best crop ever," talking about us as if we were stalks of field corn, tasseling out, soon ready for a bumper harvest.

I sat up straight in my choir-loft pew. The hymnal slid off my lap with a thud. Pastor Hedlund was introducing a handsome, young seminarian from Luther Bible Institute. He was from Indonesia, a great city called Djakarta, Pastor said. We were privileged to have him interning in our parish for the remainder of the summer. Because his last name was long and nearly impossible for a Norwegian to pronounce—he paused for chuckles from the congregation—we could call him by his first name—Asal. And, by the way, Pastor Asal would gladly accept an invitation to Sunday dinner.

The congregation laughed again on cue, demonstrating their Christian acceptance of this exotic Lutheran with his dark skin and deep black eyes who hailed from the far side of the planet.

I glanced at Mama in the pew behind me. Her eager smile told me I could plan on setting another plate at the dinner table. She had a chuck roast in the oven and two rhubarb pies baked fresh last night. The family took her efforts for granted. It would do her good to hear a little foreign praise.

Pastor Asal bowed humbly, then lifted his eyes, smiled broadly, and stepped up to the lectern. He was a broad, short man, too short to reach the microphone. Although his words were not amplified sufficiently to reach the choir loft, his voice was lyrical, transporting me across the sea to distant ports I had visited only in the pages of the *National Geographic*.

Mama seemed enchanted, too. At the end of the service she rushed after him, elbowing her sopranos aside, offering Pastor Asal the first invitation to Sunday dinner. He bowed and kissed her hand. "Thank you, Mrs. Hellerud. I am honored to accept your gracious invitation."

Daddy stood beside her, nodding and smiling hospitably. He reached for Mama's hand, something I had not seen him do in years.

Pastor Asal was charming company. He smiled and bowed and

praised his hostesses at every opportunity. We lapped it up. Mama was acting flustered and flattered. My sisters and I weren't behaving any better. We bickered about who would be seated near our courtly guest.

Susie and I easily shoved eight-year-old Priscilla aside, and she pouted at the far end of the table. We were about to plant ourselves on either side of Pastor Asal, when Peggy sidled up, wearing an anxious smile. Susie and I shot her menacing glances. She might have wilted and withdrawn, but Asal settled the dispute, choosing "the blonde princess in the yellow frock" to be seated at his side. Peggy blushed brightly. Although now seventeen, she was still reticent and awkward. Our guest could surely see that; he was only being kind.

I worried that Pastor Asal might expect a table prayer, but he did not pause or bow his head. He dug into Mama's roast beef and mashed potatoes without a single "Praise-the-Lord." Looking relieved, the family followed suit.

After dinner Pastor Asal launched into a verbal tour of the Indonesian islands.

"My country consists of more than three thousand islands in southeast Asia," he explained. "Djakarta is a large city—more than four million people—on the island of Java. It is mountainous and tropical. We don't raise corn or wheat, like you. We grow rubber and sugar, rice and coffee and tobacco. Most of our people are very poor, and they work very hard. They also love to play and sing and dance. They take time for *beauty*."

Pastor Asal looked directly at my older sister, flashing a pearly smile. He called her by her full name—Margaret Ann—which lent her a disturbing dignity.

"The world is really very small, Margaret Ann. Your Wisconsin moon also shines on Indonesia, but instead of beautifying cornstalks, it dances on the Java Sea, catching the top of every wave with a thousand tiny lights."

After half an hour of this gushing travelogue, Daddy and Teddy excused themselves. They decided it was time to clean the barn, something they never tackled on a Sunday afternoon.

Finally, Pastor Asal invited Peggy for a walk in the cow pasture, and we twins were stuck with a heap of dirty dishes.

It was so unfair. We couldn't help that Peggy had been such a wallflower all these years. Now she was making up for it in one afternoon, trying to impress a man at least ten years older. And a *minister,* for heaven's sake. Besides, I didn't like the way he was looking at her, staring at those breasts that bloomed like plump tomatoes inside her cotton sundress.

"When is he leaving, Mama?" I whined.

"Be polite, Sara," Mama warned me. "It's not every day that we have such an interesting guest."

Asal and Peggy did not return until suppertime. Mama seemed a little tense. Daddy and Teddy came in from the barn smelling of cow manure. We all sat down to sandwiches, carrot-raisin salad, and another round of pie.

"I can take you back to town," Mama began, jingling her car keys before Asal had even finished his dessert.

Asal didn't seem to hear.

"I understand that Margaret Ann plans to become a nurse. You must be proud of her unselfish goals. Perhaps she'd like to know something about the health care needs in Indonesia . . . "

By the time Mama, Daddy, and Teddy finished evening milking, it was time for baths and bed. Asal fetched the small, leather bag he had parked beside the davenport.

"This is lovely of you, Mrs. Hellerud," he crooned. "Your home is so much more comfortable than the guest room in the parsonage. I'll be quite happy right here on the living room sofa. I hope none of you hard-working people are thinking of giving up your bed for me."

Mama's dinner invitation had turned into a slumber party. She was at a rare loss for words. I helped her equip the davenport with sheets and blankets. She made neat hospital corners with a quick stab of her hand, just as the Polk County Homemakers instructed.

"There! One night. Tomorrow morning I'm taking him back to town," Mama announced primly.

Asal was in the bathroom, soaking in the claw-footed tub, while Daddy and Teddy fidgeted in the kitchen, mopping their necks with their red bandannas, spilling the chaff from the cuffs and pockets of their overalls. Their patience ran out, and they trooped up to bed, just as Asal emerged in a silk robe, perfumed and pomaded, smelling like a tropical flower.

I made a beeline for the bathroom to relieve my swollen bladder and found an array of oils and perfumes on the back of the commode. Great. Five women, two sweaty farmers, and a preacher who smelled like the Garden of Eden all sharing one tiny bathroom. This could get tiresome in a hurry.

Our guest slept soundly. We tiptoed through our household chores until midmorning when he finally arose to greet the day. Mama served a late breakfast of waffles and bacon but seemed immune to Asal's lavish praise. The men had already spent three hours in the fields, she reported. They were sweaty and exhausted. The weather man predicted it would hit at least a hundred degrees Fahrenheit by midafternoon.

Asal beamed. "We must all go swimming, to celebrate our new friendship. Let me show you some delightful water sports from Java . . . "

It sounded like a good idea, especially to those of us who missed our baths the night before. We changed into our swimming togs and piled into the De Soto. There wasn't room for everyone, so Mama claimed she didn't want to go. Peggy boldly volunteered to sit on Asal's lap.

Daddy was silent on the five-mile drive to Half Moon Lake. Daddy and Teddy looked comical dressed in swimming trunks and farmers' tans. Their red-brown necks and forearms resembled leather patches glued on their milk-white skin. Teddy waded out, cooling himself by inches. Daddy splashed near shore while his daughters frolicked with Asal near the raft. I dived deep under the water and opened my eyes to see Asal's hand stroking Peggy's thighs. He grabbed her crotch and worked his slim fingers beneath the elastic of her swim suit. I was alarmed, but mesmerized. This was a show worth drowning for. I stayed under as long as I could, then rocketed to the surface, gasping for breath.

Susie surfaced beside me. "I'm going to get Daddy," she sputtered angrily.

Daddy plowed into the water and torpedoed to the raft. "That's enough. We're going home," was all he said.

Peggy sat meekly next to Daddy in the front seat. Asal retreated to the rear.

Mama had hamburgers and potato salad waiting, and we nibbled politely.

"I have a trip to town right after lunch, and Pastor Hedlund is expecting you," she announced to Asal. He headed toward the bathroom to collect his toiletries.

Our parents retreated to their bedroom for a hasty conference. I heard part of their discussion from behind the bedroom door.

"Get that Pastor Ass-Hole out of here!" Daddy whispered hoarsely, "before I punch him all the way to China, or wherever the hell he comes from."

"Indonesia," Mama corrected him sternly. "Now calm down, Harvey. What on earth happened out at the lake to upset you like this?"

I could not hear his reply. Soon they emerged from the bedroom, a united front, with puckered lips and furrowed foreheads. They were clearly worried that one of their precious cornstalks was about to be detassled—by a man with olive skin and thick, black hair. Really, they could be so provincial. On the other hand, I thought they might be right. This might be dangerous for Peggy. She was so high strung, so gullible and inexperienced. I wanted to be open-minded, yet I shared my parents' anger and concern.

Peggy had not heard a thing. "Sara!" she confided excitedly, "I'm going to let you in on a secret, but you must promise not to tell."

I followed her into the pantry. She didn't wait for me to cross my heart. "Asal is asking for my hand."

"It seems to me he is after more than just your hand," I said.

"You don't get it. He wants to marry me. I'll be out of this cow town before you know it! I know I'm awfully young, but Asal says that early marriages are common there. They need nurses desperately, with all the typhus and malaria, so I can serve the Lord that way. Asal thinks God has ordained it."

She was serious. I was shocked and frightened for my sister. Peggy could be difficult, but I was not ready to see her spirited away by a perfumed little preacher who did not even pray at the table. Was he a Christian minister at all? He could be an imposter, enticing innocent blonde farm girls like our Peggy into slavery in the steamy tropics on the opposite side of the globe. She might be picking rubber or tobacco for the rest of her dismal life. Or she might simply disappear.

It was my turn to tattle.

Without further commotion, Daddy whisked our friend away to town. His summer internship at Milltown Evangelical was canceled. We never spoke of him again.

Peggy remained with us a while longer. By fall she was a sassy high school senior.

"Now that you two brats are freshmen, I suppose I'll be running into you in the hallways of Milltown High. Well, don't ask me to help you find your way around, and don't expect to borrow any clothes!"

Sometimes Susie and I wished she were on a boat bound for worlds unknown. Mostly we were glad to see her safe and happy, looking forward to her nursing career.

A crew-cut neighbor boy named Spike McCurdy invited Peggy to the Prom. The seniors had chosen *South Pacific* as their theme, promising to transform the gymnasium into a tropical paradise.

Peggy had no time to help her classmates beautify the gym. She had to work some magic on herself. She wrapped her body in yards of sky-blue taffeta and nylon netting and paraded through the house. She sketched and measured, cut and sewed, creating a ball gown fit for Cinderella. Finally she glued a clutch of rhinestones all across the skirt, predicting they would twinkle on the dance floor like a thousand tiny lights.

The Polk County Homewreckers

Aside from church, Mama was never much of a joiner. She had one affiliation—the Polk County Homemakers. She saved her ten-year membership award—a framed certificate representing ten years of monthly meetings devoted to lessons in family nutrition, budget-wise shopping, emergency first aid, home nursing, bread baking, party planning, cleaning, canning, vegetable gardening, slipcovering, stain removal, and various other skills demanded by a family in the 1950s.

The Homemakers' Creed is printed on the back:

> We, the Homemakers of Wisconsin, believe in the sanctity of the *home*, the cradle of character, blessed by motherly devotion and guarded by fatherly protection.
>
> *We pledge ourselves:*
>
> To work for the preservation and improvement of home and community life;

To strive for healthier minds and bodies, and better living;

To promote the welfare of our boys and girls, the nation's greatest asset;

To be true to God and country, and of lasting service to our homes and communities.

"Mama's off to her Homewreckers meeting," Daddy joked the only night of the month when Mama could not be found at home. That fourth Thursday evening she always hurried with the barn chores, scrubbed her arms and neck and face, changed into a dress, nylon hose and pumps, arranged her hair, and applied a dash of powder and some bright, red lipstick. Then she jumped into the car and sped down the driveway, clouds of dust billowing in her wake.

It would be ten o'clock before she arrived home, all coffeed up and too excited to sleep. Our parents' late-night conversation funneled upstairs to our bedroom through the hot-air vent, and my sisters and I strained to catch any tidbits that might provoke our interest.

"What was the topic tonight?" Daddy asked, sounding half asleep.

Mama shared the latest word on making beds with tidy hospital corners or removing blood or food stains from cotton, wool, or acetate. Daddy was snoring loudly, long before the lesson was over.

Mama brought home mimeographed "lessons" from her Homemaker meetings. Sometimes she shared them with her daughters. "Last night's lesson was all about housecleaning, using the new products to advantage. You girls are all going to be keeping house some day. And I'm counting on you to help me now as much as you possibly can. You really ought to read this."

I skimmed it, feigning interest.

Spring housecleaning has bitten the dust. The American housewife can keep her household tasks constantly under control by using the modern methods which are now available. She has Big Business to thank for this. Post-war industry has concentrated on the needs of the housewife and supplied us with many "hands" in the way of household equipment. With a whole battery of tools at her command—light weight vacuum cleaners, brooms, brushes, and cellulose sponges of every size and description—the American housewife is turning housecleaning into a very specialized skill.

She can select from a wide range of nationally distributed household products—from gentle soaps and detergents such as Dreft or Ivory Flakes to heavy duty Fels Naptha, Duz, or Oxydol. She has Soilex for her soiled walls and Bab-O for the bathtub.

The new products take so much of the drudgery out of cleaning that the modern homemaker can wear a poplin housedress while she goes about these tasks, looking relaxed and attractive for unexpected visitors. She notes industry's discovery that bending requires 43% more energy than standing straight—and chooses a long-handled dustpan. She hears that U.S. soldiers do better on the march with a ten minute rest interval every hour—and she rests before she gets tired. She invents techniques: dust mitts for both hands to speed dusting; a small open market basket with handle to carry cans of paste and bottles of polish from room to room. The many-handed woman takes still another tip from industry and does her cleaning day by day instead of letting it pile up on her. Result: a happy housewife and spring freshness in the home all year around.

What a joke, I thought. Mama was a many-handed woman all right. She had eight hands in all, and six of them belonged to her daughters. This lesson was completely useless. Mama was plenty efficient all by herself, using nothing but her own two hands and a bit of elbow grease. She never needed a ten-minute break, and a pair of mittens would have slowed her down.

Some Homewreckers' lessons on basic cooking might have been more helpful. While Mama turned out delicious breads and pastries and could also spread a tasty Sunday dinner, those three squares a day were usually handled in a slapdash fashion. She admitted she wished cooking were a seasonal chore—like breaking sod or whitewashing the barn. Once done, it ought to stay done for a year or so. Those relentless, pesky mealtimes kept sneaking up on her, three times a day, when she was knee-deep in something more important—mending fences, cultivating corn.

When the noon whistle blew in town, Mama raced to the house, fired up the range, grabbed a package of meat out of the freezer compartment of the refrigerator, and beat it with a wooden mallet. She heated the cast-iron skillet to a white-hot glow and plopped in a tablespoon of Crisco, along with the partially defrosted hunks of cow. Oil splattered in all directions. The hot pan sizzled in protest. Those steaks were tough to begin with, harvested as they were from aging Holsteins well beyond their prime. Now they would be served up on our plates, black on the outside, crunchy with ice crystals sparkling within. I was always puzzled why diners would order anything as disagreeable as "steak" when they visited a restaurant and actually had a choice.

A couple of side dishes helped to balance this large dose of protein. There was always bread, of course. And there might be Jell-O or a carrot-raisin salad on the side. Mama might haul out last evening's mashed potatoes and fry them up in the same black skillet that produced our charcoaled meat.

No time was given to pleases or thank yous or complaints;

within ten minutes chairs were pushed back from the table, and the room was empty. Only a cloud of oily smoke hung over the kitchen range to remind us that another meal had come and gone.

Cleaning up the dishes became my job from the age of eight until I escaped for good. Mama did not pass any dishwashing lessons on to me, but I'd been observing the routine long enough. I must haul buckets of ice-cold water from the well pump, then heat it on the kitchen range. I must scrape the dishes carefully, saving the scraps for the barn cats. I must dipper the water into my basin, as sparingly as possible. Soap flakes were precious, too. If there were any suds at all, I knew I had used too much. Sometimes I conserved energy as well by skipping the washing process altogether, simply sponging the plates with a greasy, soggy towel. Mama usually caught me taking shortcuts. She despaired for my future. What kind of wife could I be when I was unable to handle even this most elementary household task?

As for cooking, I never graduated beyond Jell-O brand chocolate pudding. I loved to measure out the milk, mix and stir till it was smooth, then watch it come to the boiling point. I stirred and tasted and stirred some more, lifting my kettle just in time as the pudding crawled up the sides and threatened to flow over the edge onto the hot burner. My pudding was always a perfect consistency, never burned or lumpy. I sampled often from my wooden spoon and also ate the skin that formed on the individual serving dishes once I had portioned it out. I was usually too full of pudding to eat a proper meal, and the remaining servings were small, but no one seemed to notice.

The Homewreckers probably talked about child rearing, too. They must have recommended praising children, helping them build pride and self-esteem.

"Sara makes wonderful chocolate pudding!" Mama bragged repeatedly. Yet she never offered to teach me further culinary skills. She was just too busy, I guess.

Time was precious so we specialized. Peggy was assistant cook. She also sewed and mended. Susie liked to straighten, mop, and dust. There was nothing important left for me except starching, sprinkling, and ironing—and those endless piles of dirty dishes.

We were all pressed into service on laundry day. Mama scheduled this on Mondays during the summer months but switched to Saturdays during the school year so she would have plenty of help. Beginning right after breakfast, we emptied mounds of soiled clothing from boxes and baskets in the four upstairs bedrooms. We stripped beds down to the mattress ticking. We lifted the barn overalls, stiff with straw and manure, from their pegs on the porch. All were sorted and stacked around the kitchen according to a complicated method based on color, fabric, and aroma. I never quite mastered the sorting rules and was constantly in trouble.

"What are you doing with those piles, Sara?"

"I'm sorting them with my foot. I read somewhere that bending down takes almost twice the energy."

"This job takes all your energy, young lady. I suggest you bend—or squat right down—and work with both your hands. No, not like that! Never put bright colors with pastels—especially nothing red. You will turn everything pink with that load, mark my word. And never mix delicates like those underpants in with the denims. Be sure to check for stains—the stained ones get soaked with Rinso in the basin. Be quick now. I'm almost ready for another load of whites." I loathed the basin duty, which included hand scrubbing food and blood spots and other stubborn stains. Since I was less than thorough, Peggy was usually assigned this task.

Usually I ended up with the simple job of rounding up the hose, connecting it to the well pump, and trailing it across the yard and into the enclosed back porch, which served as a laundry room on Saturdays. The water was rusty. Because the well had been sunk so close to the silo pit, the water took on a yellow hue and smelled of silage in the fall. It wouldn't do for the rinse cycle. Both rinse tubs—the same tubs that served for our Saturday night baths—were filled from large milk cans containing clean, clear water that Daddy hauled from town.

Mama supervised filling the machine with the right amount of cold water mixed with hot from a large copper boiler on the stove. She also dumped in carefully measured Oxydol and the first load of whites. We took turns stirring with a wooden stick, fishing the laundry out of its steaming bath, running it through the wringer, rinsing, wringing, rinsing and bluing, wringing again, hauling it out, and pegging it to the clothesline. I didn't mind the morning hours but grew restless and tired by midday, when we started washing towels and colored shirts. By three o'clock we had progressed to greasy overalls and foul-smelling barn pants. The water was disgusting—gray-blue and thick enough to float the bits of chaff and cow manure that agitated to the surface. The heavy snaps and buckles often caught in the wringer, causing it to fly apart and hold up the entire operation while Mama made repairs.

Peggy was rewarded for her speed and skill with a relatively cheery task—gathering in the clothespins and the dry, sweet-smelling laundry. On a bright, breezy day, the fresh clothing smelled of sunshine and clover. She sniffed and sighed as she passed by. Peggy did not have it quite so good in winter. Mama helped her then. Most of the hanging was done indoors on twine strings strung in the hall and stairwell and through every downstairs room. Only the heaviest overalls were hung out on the line. They were gathered up quite frozen, almost stiff enough to hike in on their own.

Susie and I drained the tubs at day's end. We were revolted to see the cold, soupy water draining from the tubs through the long hose into the backyard. The last of it had to be toted out in buckets, the sludge wiped from the bottom of the tubs and discarded far away, beyond the borders of our tidy lawn. And even though Mama always checked the pockets and demanded that we do the same, there were the inevitable nuts and bolts and screws and God-knows-what-men-keep-in-their-pockets that had to be fished out of the hoses and drains. I was always impressed by the amount of dirt a family of seven could collect in one week's time. Impressed and exhausted.

"There now, doesn't that make you feel good?" Mama exclaimed.

"Sure does," her helpers chorused wearily.

We sat down to Mama's pancake supper, almost too tired to eat. No meat or potatoes were served on laundry day. We didn't mind. It kept kitchen clean-up to a minimum.

The laundry routine was somewhat simpler once we moved to the Milltown farm in 1953 where there was indoor plumbing and hot running water. But except for the filling and draining, we continued to fight with the same old galvanized rinsing tubs, the same pokey wringer machine.

"Those new automatics just can't get your clothes as clean! They're fine for city folks, I suppose—but you can't tell me they were designed to handle mud and manure," Mama insisted, defending her ancient but dependable equipment. "I'm going to stick with my wringer machine—I don't care what the Homemakers say."

By the late 1950s many of the Homemakers were "working out," earning hourly wages outside the home. The monthly lessons began to emphasize self-fulfillment. They promoted electric appliances for the homemaker, which would free up her time and broaden her choices. Mama was not sure that they were headed in the right direction. But she remained a loyal member of that organization for ten years—until 1959. After that she just couldn't seem to find the time.

That last autumn Mama invited her family to attend the Polk

County Homemakers' Musical Revue. The star performer was Mary Jane Manson, a young, unmarried home economist, recently employed by the Polk County Extension Office. Mary Jane pranced around the stage, twirling a parasol, singing:

> Single gal, single gal,
> Around the town she flies,
> Married gal, married gal,
> Rocks and cradles and cries.
> So if you are a single gal,
> Single you should stay.
> Don't become a married gal,
> And dream your life away.

"What a song to offer a group of housewives tied down tight with farms and families!" Mama laughed, humming the catchy tune all the way home.

At the age of sixteen, I thought it was pretty good advice. If I ever did become a married gal, I wouldn't be wrestling with wood stoves and wringer washing machines. No, I'd be one of those modern types featured in the *Ladies' Home Companion*. I could picture myself already, wearing city suits, high-heeled shoes, and little white gloves, waving at my gleaming appliances as I danced out the door.

Mrs. Fleming

Mama's older sister, Adele Fleming, was a tiny woman—four foot ten—with an expansive nature more than compensating for her size. She was the only one of the nine Williamson children to pursue a college education, which her parents had promoted and financed at considerable sacrifice. Most of the Williamsons were outstanding students, and Adele was no exception. But she was born with a handicapping difference—four fingers on each hand.

My siblings and I adored this cheerful, thumbless aunty. She had married and moved to California when we were small but vacationed in Wisconsin nearly every summer, always bringing hugs and laughter. Each year we displayed school report cards, poems and paintings, music and dancing, all our best work from the previous year for Aunty Adele to admire.

She was sincere and generous in her praise.

"That's a fine essay on soil conservation, Sara. Sharp, short sentences, well organized, and very well expressed. I hope your teacher noticed that. At any rate, you'd get an A from me."

An A rating from Aunty Adele was no small thing. She had been teaching in a private school for many years in glamorous North Hollywood, California. She taught wealthy students, children of the stars—Bing Crosby's daughter, Debbie Reynolds's son. We relished her descriptions of these privileged kids. Her brisk assessments puffed us up with pride.

"They're no prettier, no brighter than the kids in Milltown, Wisconsin," she told our mother. "And most of them are awfully spoiled. They don't know how to work. I don't have a single student who can write like Sara or play the piano as well as Susie. I've had enough of California. I'd love to come back to the Midwest to teach, where we still have solid values, where kids still want to read and write and learn."

The timing was fortunate. Unity High School needed a teacher qualified for English, speech, and drama. Adele Fleming applied and got the job. Susie and I were sitting in her sophomore English class on August 28, 1958, when she entered the room for the first time, outfitted in a trim suit and spike heels that raised her height to five foot two.

"Good morning!" she exclaimed. "I am your English teacher, Mrs. Fleming." She wiped the blackboard clean and chalked her name in expansive, loopy letters—Adele Clarice Fleming—then faced the class and gave us Hamlet's monologue.

> To be or not to be, that is the question
> Whether it is nobler in the mind to suffer
> The slings and arrows of outrageous fortune
> Or take up arms against a sea of troubles
> And by opposing, end them . . .

Her students came to attention at their desks, eyes opened wide. Already they were suffering the slings and arrows of classic drama and were not opposing it a bit.

Susie and I were surprised by our aunt's flamboyance in the classroom. The dynamo who charged up and down the aisles was not our cozy little aunt; this was Mrs. Fleming—teacher, actress, and philosopher—someone we would have to share.

Before long it became obvious to the faculty of Unity High School that Mrs. Fleming held philosophies quite different from their own. They were firmly convinced that rewards should be offered sparingly, that praise and recognition were of no value unless they were hard won in advance. Mrs. Fleming turned this formula around. She was generous with her trust, encouragement, and high expectations, certain that worthy performance would follow. She doled out lavish praise at the first sign of a sincere effort. Her grading curve, like her penmanship, looped high and wide. She entertained and dramatized, perched on table tops, waving her arms, or paced the classroom, ranging far from desk and podium. Sometimes she hugged enthusiastic students who lingered at her door until the final bell called them, reluctant and tardy, to their next classes.

By midterm most of Mrs. Fleming's students were earning A's and B's, some for the first time ever. They made a sport of English grammar and competed at diagramming complex sentences in record time. They learned to love Shakespeare, Milton, Whitman, Sandburg, Robert Frost. They recited pages of *Macbeth* or *Spoon River Anthology* from memory.

Every Monday morning Mrs. Fleming wrote a favorite quotation on the blackboard; by Friday many students had committed these to heart.

> It is better to know some of the questions than all of the answers.—James Thurber
>
> Life shrinks or expands according to one's courage.—Anais Nin
>
> Most of the shadows of this life are caused by standing in one's own sunshine.—Ralph Waldo Emerson
>
> Education is not the filling of a pail, but the lighting of a fire.—William Butler Yeats
>
> Art washes the dust of everyday life from the soul.—Pablo Picasso
>
> What is laid down, ordered, factual, is never enough to embrace the whole truth; life always spills over the rim of every cup.—Boris Pasternak

It was exciting stuff. Mrs. Fleming's students began repeating her favorite quotations and classroom dialogues at the supper table.

"Mrs. Fleming tells us to keep questioning everything we read and hear, including the radio, newspaper, our parents, teachers, presidents, even priests and ministers. She says the purpose of an education is learning to think for yourself."

"Mrs. Fleming says it is important to know what you think and don't be afraid to say it. You can always change your mind, she says. The biggest mistake is not taking the time to be informed, not bothering to have an opinion at all."

"I think Mrs. Fleming is right—everyone should study at least two world religions besides their own. And she doesn't mean

Methodists and Baptists—she means *Buddhism* or *Hinduism!*"

"She says she thinks it's perfectly okay for Lutheran kids to date the Catholics . . . that we are more alike than we are different."

Now and then we heard the parents' worried talk at church gatherings or at the grocery store.

"The woman's divorced, you know. Lived fifteen years in California and came back with some pretty strange ideas."

"Maybe so, but you have to give her credit. It's amazing how that tiny person can control a classroom of rowdy seniors, right up to graduation day."

"Well I don't know . . . "

"They say she never has to raise her voice. She wouldn't weigh a hundred pounds soaking wet with a rock in her pocket."

"All the same, her liberal California notions might not be what we need in the long run. She is certainly making it tough for the rest of the teachers to run a tight ship. I worry about the future. Someone really needs to rein her in."

But it was difficult to discount prizewinning essays, dramas, and orations or the new trophy case filling up with plaques brought home by the forensics and debating teams. In spite of mild warnings from the principal, Mrs. Fleming continued with her own eccentric methods. Certainly the best efforts of our other teachers paled when compared with the wit and fervor of this woman who loved literature—and her students—without restraint.

Susie and I found we did not mind sharing our favorite aunt with the entire high school. We realized we had been lucky. Aunty Adele had been working her sorcery with us since we were toddlers. She had cocked her head and sighed and laughed, enraptured by our every clever word. It was fun to sit back now and watch her mesmerize our classmates. We noticed that she targeted especially needy students, one at a time, like a fairy godmother with a powerful wand.

The spring of our junior year she selected ten unlikely boys to act as whalers in a one-act drama by Eugene O'Neill. Susie played the captain's wife, the lone female aboard ship, who went insane after years on the high seas. In the final devastating scene, Susie cackled, screamed hysterically, and thundered minor chords on a broken-down organ as the hulking whalers stood helplessly behind her, tears streaming from their eyes. The cast won a standing ovation and later a state drama trophy that rivaled anything the football team had yet delivered.

The debating team captured a handsome trophy when they traveled all the way to Madison to argue whether "It Is Better to Be Red than Dead." That lively debate, broadcast on radio, continued across dinner tables and in the streets of Milltown and Polk County for weeks to come.

During our senior year it was Jerry Bibeau's turn to shine. Transplanted from St. Paul, Minnesota, the previous year, Jerry was tough, streetwise, lonely, and unwilling—or unable—to find friends among his rural classmates. He swaggered through the halls and used city slang and crude profanity. He bragged about his appetite for sex and liquor and his run-ins with the law, wherever he could find an audience. Bolder girls were intrigued by his bravado, his tall, muscular build, wavy brown hair, dark brooding eyes, the pack of Camels rolled into the left sleeve of his T-shirt.

Jerry had a deep, resonant voice, an attribute not lost on Mrs. Fleming. She assigned him a front-row seat in senior English. She called on Jerry often to read aloud in class, marveling at his fine speaking voice, his clear enunciation. Halfway through the year, Jerry prepared and delivered an original oration on the French explorers in Wisconsin. He won a regional competition.

"I hope you will consider a career in broadcasting!" Mrs. Fleming exclaimed. "A voice like that is a gift that should be shared with the wider world."

He beamed. I noticed Jerry was even more appealing when he smiled.

His grades improved, not only in English but in geometry, chemistry, and American government. By the third quarter he achieved the honor roll.

The Drama Club selected *A Man Called Peter* for their winter production, and Jerry won the starring role. During the weeks of rehearsal that followed, Jerry became Peter Marshall, gentle, loving, and courageous. I became his Catherine on and off the stage. He was calm and respectful, even when we were alone in his rusted '51 Chevy. I forgot to wonder what had become of the cynical, young hoodlum I had avoided for so long.

One evening Jerry drove me to a cabin near Half Moon Lake to meet his father, explaining that his mother had long ago disappeared from his life. Jerry's father was a small, swarthy man, nearly toothless, older than his years. He straightened up as we appeared and held out his whiskey bottle in a hearty greeting.

"No, thanks, Dad," said Jerry. "Sara doesn't drink. We'll have some Coke."

We drank our Cokes and tried to make casual conversation. I asked Jerry's father if he'd be attending the class play.

"Nah," he said thickly, "I'm not much for town doings anymore."

So Jerry would have no family to share his proudest night.

The play was an enormous success. Even the bleachers overflowed. We made three curtain calls.

That summer, right after graduation, Jerry left for California, joking that he felt lucky enough to break into movies. After all, he looked like Jimmy Dean. Everyone raved about his acting talent and his golden voice. He promised he would write.

I never heard from him again.

Two years later, during my Christmas break from college, Aunty Adele told me she had received a note from Mr. Bibeau, thanking her for Jerry's senior year, the best time of his life. California had not worked out. He couldn't land a job. He'd drifted into drugs and alcohol, and on Thanksgiving Day he'd armed himself against a sea of troubles. He'd stuck a gun inside his mouth and pulled the trigger.

"Oh, no!" I gasped. "How could this happen?"

"I'm partially responsible," she mourned. "I built his hopes so terribly high. He never found the sunshine that I promised him—never caught a single glimpse of it."

"That can't have anything to do with you."

"I'm old and tired—maybe the world changed when I wasn't looking. I had no right to promise him so much."

Toward spring Aunty Adele announced her early retirement. A brief interview appeared in the *Polk County Ledger.* She was quoted in the final paragraph: "I have been privileged to teach many eager, talented young people at Unity High. It was important work, teaching the future leaders of this land. I hope to have many visits from former students during my retired years."

Privately she complained that students were becoming unruly, disrespectful, that they were no longer eager to learn. Her magic was too small these days. The greatest poets and playwrights failed to stir them. The Drama Club wanted to produce nothing but light-weight comedies, and she had been unable to recruit a single student for debate this year. If even Wisconsin had been poisoned by greed and sloth and too much television, then the whole society, from coast to coast, was going straight to hell. We wouldn't have to worry any more about the Russians taking over—we would engineer our own defeat.

Growing old was battle enough. She was suffering from migraine headaches and gastric ulcers. Oh, teaching still offered small rewards, but they were just too few and far between.

I wondered if the students had really changed so much, or whether the teacher had lost heart and energy. Some of each, perhaps.

I wondered who would take her place at Unity High. They would need another dynamo—someone waving a wand of possibilities, urging students to ask the big questions, promising that life can spill over the rim of every cup.

Constellations

Dedicated as she was to dairying, Mama was the natural manager of operations. She assessed the work load, made assignments, set the deadlines, and reviewed performance, often critically. Daddy engineered our recreation, such as movies, Sunday drives without a known destination, ice cream cones, and other small rewards.

This well-established pattern had a curious exception: when it came to Susie's musical endeavors, our parents traded roles. Daddy took a fresh interest in the choring schedule while Mama claimed that lessons, contests, and recitals must take precedence.

"I know it's haying season, Harvey. If this Minneapolis Aquatennial piano competition weren't so crucial for Susan, I wouldn't think of taking time off now. But a win like this could mean important recognition and a scholarship."

Daddy was supportive and agreeable. He had been making the seventy-mile trip to Minneapolis nearly every Saturday for the past year so Susie could study piano at MacPhail School of Music. Susie's lessons with a well-respected teacher, Mrs. Cleo Hiner, had been encouraged by Grandma Launsby. ("You need to begin studying with someone in the city, Darling. You need a teacher who can introduce you to influential people there and put you into competitions. Playing well is not enough. You'll have to win some attention in order to further your career.") And so Susie's weekly lessons at MacPhail had commenced, despite tuition costs and transportation obstacles. As Mama said, preparing for a musical career demanded sacrifice. She had not been able to afford such costly dreams herself, but she could make them happen for a gifted daughter.

"Teddy should be able to manage evening chores. Henry Johnson up the road has promised to check in and see if Ted needs any help. And we can count on Peggy to mind the house and watch Priscilla," Mama said, as if to reassure herself as well as Daddy.

"Well, we'd better leave plenty early," Daddy sighed. "Four o'clock, in case of a flat tire or unexpected traffic."

The competition was scheduled for 7 P.M. We arrived at the Nicollet Hotel with over an hour to spare. Susie had time to warm up on the Steinway and get some final coaching from Mrs. Hiner. Mama greeted the Milltown folks as they arrived—several ladies from her Homemakers Club, the Lutheran pastor, and members of the choir.

Daddy paced the ballroom, watching a crew of men set up rows of metal folding chairs. I watched the backstage coaching until the audience gathered, then joined Mama and Daddy in the second row.

The curtains opened. An announcer made the usual welcoming remarks, then introduced the first of thirty-two contestants—a poised young woman of about twenty, playing a showy Rachmaninoff prelude. I wondered, briefly, if we belonged in this contest at all. Still, Mrs. Hiner knew these competitions; we had to trust her judgment. One of her students had won last year's event, and Mrs. Hiner was hoping for another victory. She had been coaching Susie on this piece for several months. Without touching the keyboard I had committed every note to aural memory.

Each performance seemed to eclipse the one before it. I felt terribly nervous for my twin.

Finally Susie walked on stage, wearing an older cousin's hand-me-down—a scoop-necked, royal-blue taffeta with white polka dots. She shrugged her shoulders, centering the too-large bodice

Chicagoland Music Festival, Class B piano competition—"First place winner is Susan Hellerud of Milltown, Wisconsin!"

on her narrow frame. She had yanked her straight blonde hair into a pony tail and fastened it with a rubber band, exactly the way she wore it when she mowed the lawn at home. Dark blue moons of perspiration rose around her armpits. Her back was stained with sweat. She looked homespun and awkward, and I hoped the country grooming would not count against her once the judges heard her play.

Feeling as if I occupied the piano bench myself, I watched Susie raise her hands to the keyboard, poised for the opening bars of Scarlatti's Sonata in G Major, Longo 387.

My fingers hovered just above my lap. Then, synchronized with Susie, I played across my pleated skirt in a lively presto, 12/8 time. The piece was technically demanding, full of forearm staccato. No hovering close to the keyboard. No damper pedal to cover the mistakes. Trills and arpeggios and rapid scales challenged the right hand; broken chords, followed by risky leaps to the bass notes, challenged the left. I had heard my twin practicing those bass leaps over and over, groaning every time she missed and landed "in the crack." Tonight we nailed each one. Every note sounded with brilliant clarity. Before the last arpeggio was played, I knew we had the prize in hand.

Five contestants later, the announcer confirmed our victory:

> Ladies and gentlemen, I am pleased to announce the first place winner of the 1958 Minneapolis Aquatennial Class B piano competition is . . . Miss Susan Hellerud of Milltown, Wisconsin!

Applause resounded through the ballroom. Then Susie was engulfed by eager fans. I edged my way through the crowd and took my place beside her.

"Hold our trophy, Sara!" I held it high and watched my twin receive a round of hugs and handshakes.

The Milltown delegation surged forward, twittering.

"Harvey and Helen! Aren't you *proud?*"

"Susan has put us on the map tonight!"

Mrs. Lindoo—wife of the Milltown pharmacist and lead soprano in the choir—complimented Daddy, gushing about his cultured family until he reddened and turned away.

She cornered me. "Here's the little twin . . . she must have talent, too. Tell me, dear, what do *you* do?"

I wanted to scream, "*Are you deaf and blind? We play the piano!*" Instead I shook my head and murmured that I was only an experienced listener.

I studied my untrained hands in amazement. A tide of comprehension walled away since early childhood came crashing over me: Susie won her victories independently. My sense of musical accomplishment was a complete delusion; I had not learned to play a single note.

During the long ride home Mama twisted around to chatter with Susie, who sat beside me in the back seat of the De Soto. They planned for the next level of competition, which would be the Chicagoland Music Festival in August. There was a thousand-dollar scholarship at stake. The contest would be held at McCormick Place, an enormous conference center said to be the largest single structure in the world. Susie plotted her practice schedule, with Mama's anxious approval. Let's see, it would take two weeks to polish Chopin's Fantaisie Impromtu. The Scarlatti was as nearly perfect as she could make it, but she must allow some time each day to keep the piece in her fingers. Then, of course, there would be one full month spent learning and memorizing the first movement of the Beethoven Sonata, opus 2, no. 3. Those rapid double thirds in the right hand were a special challenge. Susie would have to be excused from dishes and Saturday cleaning and lawn mowing until the contest was behind her. The other kids would be good about taking up the slack.

Then there was the matter of a suitable dress—actually two or three of them—since Susie must go to Chicago prepared for an additional performance in case of victory. The winners would perform in Soldier Field and later attend a reception at the Conrad Hilton in their honor. Mama knew it could be cool and windy in Chicago, even during August. At least one dress should have long sleeves or a little jacket . . . she'd have to study the pattern books, order the fabric, and start pedaling her Singer right away.

Daddy was not joining these discussions. He drove on through the breezy evening, cranked his window all the way down as if to suck in some badly needed air. Hair whipped our faces.

"Please, Harvey! The girls' hair!" Mama protested, clapping her own curls to either side of her head.

"It's okay. I like it," I said loudly from the back seat, suddenly realizing that I had not spoken a word since we left the Nicollet Hotel.

Daddy compromised. He rolled his window halfway up, then opened the side vent, creating a loud whistling sound that hampered any further conversation.

We finally arrived home at half-past eleven. Teddy, Peggy, and Priscilla had gone to bed, leaving a note on the kitchen table. A bulging heifer named Doris was due to drop her calf; they had penned her in the box stall with plenty of water and an ample bed of straw.

Daddy went to the barn for a final check. I followed awkwardly behind.

Doris was restless, shifting from one foot to the other, but her labor was not progressing very fast. Daddy figured she would not be needing him for several hours.

I could see Mama and Susie outlined in the kitchen window, drinking their tea, leaning toward each other at the table in eager conversation. Daddy and I lingered near the barn. It was cool and clear. The stars were brilliant in the cloudless sky.

"The North Star," I said, pointing out its steady beam. "And that must be Mars, with that reddish glow. . . . I never could see Orion, the Hunter, could you, Daddy? Or that imaginary bear? I wonder if some astronomer didn't dream them up for fun, hoping to confuse us all for centuries."

"Maybe so. There's one we can't confuse—the Big Dipper," Daddy said, connecting its seven points with his thick forefinger.

I gazed at the paired stars forming the vessel and the graceful

Susie resting after an exhausting piano competition in Minneapolis, 1958; seated on the sofa are Sara, Helen, and Grandma Launsby

three-point handle adding weight and balance. It was a perfect constellation. If even one star shifted its position, the dipper would tip and spill or fly apart, perhaps go twirling toward another galaxy.

Daddy stepped closer and slid his arm around my shoulders. I reached up to pat his hand.

"You're okay, kid. You're okay," he said, clearing his throat.

We stood awhile.

Later, I dawdled in the bathroom. By the time I finally climbed the stairway to our bedroom, Susie was sound asleep. I looked at her limp body, still as a stringless puppet on top of the covers, and felt a stunning loss.

The threat of separation had been present always. I remembered the rag dolls Daddy gave us on our fifth birthday—identical, with gangly limbs, ropey blonde hair, and embroidered smiles. Susie named her doll Lava, after Grandma Williamson. My doll was Aggie, for Grandma Hellerud who had died just before we turned four. Aggie's button eyes were set a little wider, just like mine, a lucky feature that helped us keep them separate.

About a week after our birthday, Susie came down with measles but stubbornly refused to stay in bed. Daddy punished her by hiding Lava in the basement coal bin two long days and nights. Susie's doll came back imperfect, with a coal stain on her flat white face. Susie washed her doll with Lan-O-Sheen and nearly rubbed its forehead raw. The smudge was permanent and deep.

"It doesn't matter what I do," she sobbed. "My doll will never be as good as yours."

"We'll trade," I said.

"No!" Susie screamed, snatching back her blemished doll. "Daddy thinks *I* am the spoiled kid. This ruined one belongs to me." Even then we felt the fundamental difference: Susie was born bolder and fiercer than I. She led the way, laughing louder, climbing higher, falling farther, suffering greater pain and punishment.

She also struggled harder for redemption; the piano was her instrument of grace. She had won praise and accolades, especially from Mama. Daddy must have felt compelled to balance the equation; the harder Susie worked, the more he shifted his applause to me.

Through all the years my twin and I had fought to keep our equilibrium. Now we occupied opposing corners of a tense quadrangle. I felt that we were pinned in place indefinitely.

Time flies you say? Ah no!
Time stays; 'tis we who go.
7/20/58

Dear Mugsy—

I know I haven't written you for nearly a month. The time has really gotten away from me.

I have exciting news: last Sunday evening Susan won the Minneapolis Aquatennial piano competition. She will compete in Chicago late in August and perform in Soldier Field. She won a $100 scholarship as part of this award, and will also be playing at Lake Harriet a week from tomorrow night. Last Monday night she gave a full length recital at MacPhail School of Music to open Mrs. Hiner's piano workshop. She made us all so proud. There were 22 people from Milltown at the MacPhail recital, as well as several friends and relatives from Lindstrom and Minneapolis. Quite a good turnout for a little girl from the country!

Sara started working as a waitress at the Mill Inn the week after school was out and has done very well at it. She gets only 75 cents per hour, but brings home enough in tips so that she is making close to $50 per week. Not bad when there are no transportation or living costs involved. She will be able to pay over half of her first year's college expenses, which is a big lift for us.

Susan feels she should be working like Sara to help earn money for college, but preparing for this Chicago contest is a job in itself and it is an opportunity she can't pass up. I'm hoping Harvey can go with her on this trip. Susan needs some time with him, and Harvey needs rewards and reminders that the farming has all been worth it. They can take the train straight through from the Union Station in St. Paul. Ted and I will stay home and take care of the crops and livestock.

I'll be writing again soon to let you know how all this turns out.

Love,

Helen and family

Publicity

Susie's musical success in Minneapolis and Chicago won wide publicity, including stories in the *Minneapolis Star* and the *Chicago Sun-Times*.

Another article in *Our Young People*, a newspaper for the Luther Leaguers of America, gave her national exposure. Susie and I were featured on the front page of the November 2, 1958, issue beneath a bold black headline: "First Place Winner at Chicagoland." Susie was pictured at the piano, her hands curved over the keyboard, her admiring twin at her side. "Sara watches the technique of her prize winning sister," the caption stated. The text below described Susie's recent victory in gushing detail:

> Susan is the pianist. In July she competed against thirty-two other contestants at the Minneapolis Aquatennial and won first in the class B division with a Scarlatti Sonata. Her prizes were a $100 scholarship, a trophy, and a trip to Chicago to compete in the Chicagoland Music Festival August 23. When asked who was going with her to Chicago she answered, "Just about the whole town—but not Sara. Someone has to stay home and cook!" Actually she was accompanied by her mother, her teacher, Mrs. Cleo Hiner of

Sara watching her prize-winning sister

> MacPhail Music School in Minneapolis, and two aunts visiting from California. . . .
>
> There were 29 young people trying for first place in the Class B piano division, and Susan sat in the contest room from 8 a.m. till almost 3 p.m. with nothing but a glass of milk and a roll at noon. She played at 2 p.m.
>
> She won first place!
>
> How did it feel to win? "It didn't matter too much," Sue says. "I was still Sue Hellerud. . . . "
>
> The Saturday night program at Soldier's [*sic*] Field was also exciting. Bob Hope, Herb Shriner, and other famous personalities entertained, as did the winners of the various contests. It was a wonderful experience for a young girl from a small town in northern Wisconsin . . .

A photo on the inside page showed us dressed in pedal pushers and short-sleeved blouses. Susie was steering the Minneapolis

Moline, which had been carefully positioned in front of the silo. I followed closely, one hand resting on the wheel, one hand on the gearshift of the John Deere. The Holsteins had been rounded up for background scenery. The caption read: "Susan, left, and Sara try their hand at the tractors. They have grown up in a bewildering whirl of activity among chickens, sheep, cows, tractors, automobiles, farm machinery, have been busy in school, Luther League, Sunday school, church, and yet have found time for diligent practice and study in the lovely home on the Hellerud farm."

Mama enjoyed the publicity. She reminded me that this article would be read by thousands of Luther Leaguers throughout the U.S.A. We were a testimonial to hard work and clean living.

"Lovely farm home!" I said peevishly. "It's square as a crate, without a bush or tree in sight."

"It doesn't hurt to varnish up the truth a little."

"Bewildering whirl! Chickens, too! Such silly lies. Except for your bantam roosters, we haven't raised chickens on this farm since before I was born, thank God for small favors. And that tractor scene was such a farce."

"A harmless one," said Mama. "It's a darling photograph. Those fellows were professionals, that's for sure."

"They used me like a prop—just like the Holsteins and the John Deere and the Moline! This is Susie's story—it has nothing to do with me. Why couldn't they just leave me out of it?"

Mama sighed impatiently. "Come on now, it does, too. If the rest of you kids hadn't been such a good help to us, Susie wouldn't have had all that time to work at the piano."

Mama wasn't looking; she was busy whipping lumps of thickening out of her vegetable-beef stew. Daddy saw my angry tears.

"You're not a prop, you know," he said that evening as I helped him sweep and lime the cattle walks. "Not for your twin sister, not for anyone. You'll find your niche. There's plenty of useful things to do in this world besides playing the piano."

"Or farming," I said warily.

"Yes. Farming. It can swallow you. You forget there's a whole big world out there unless you wiggle loose now and then, travel beyond your own fence line. And joke a little. Now, don't you think those journalists from Augsburg Publishing were funnier than hell? Remember how they pranced through the barn yard in their city shoes, trying to round up and pose those frisky heifers? God knows I could never get those critters to move the way I wanted 'em to either."

I had to smile. "How about that compliment as they were leaving?"

Daddy clasped his hands and mimicked, "Mr. Hellerud, I do envy you this simple country life. So close to nature. Just you and your loved ones, this rich earth, and God's own creatures, seven days a week, the year around. No worries, no pressure. What a blessed way to live."

His voice lurched through the performance, choking with laughter. He turned abruptly then and walked into the feed room. I began to follow but retreated when I saw his lowered head, his forearm braced against the concrete wall.

Sweet Corn Queen

Susie urged me to enter Milltown's beauty pageant the following summer, insisting it was my turn for the spotlight.

"You're so pretty and friendly—you'd make a super queen!"

"We're identical—remember?"

"But I'm not popular like you. I spend all my spare time at the piano—and I want to—but it costs me lots of fun and friends."

I couldn't argue. While we had both been active in the high school band and chorus and numerous activities, Susie had little spare time for teenage fun. She missed the football games, sock hops, and pajama parties and held no summer job in town. I enjoyed those things without her. Still, her sacrifices were rewarded by trophies and scholarships in Minneapolis and Chicago—much more impressive than a rhinestone crown.

By 1959 I felt ready for my share of recognition, but I was not sure this was the kind I craved. I remembered Peggy's caustic comments, thinking that she could be right. A year of nursing school in Minneapolis had broadened her perspectives. She thought the very notion of a Milltown monarch was ridiculous. Feed mills and silos were our only castles. We roamed the countryside in pickup trucks; there were no prancing steeds or golden coaches here. Did I really want to reign over a town as crude and common as this? She had a point. Furthermore the pageant was no measurement of charm or talent. There were only three requirements: contestants must be single females, sixteen years of age, and employed by local businesses. Of course a pretty face and figure helped.

It was that unofficial rule that challenged me.

I entered, sponsored by the Swirley Top drive-in where I was working as a summer car-hop. My five competitors were grocery checkers, waitresses, and soda jerks. The queen would be selected by means of grainy photos and a ballot published in the *Milltown Advertiser*; the contestant with the largest clan of relatives to stuff the ballot box at Lindoo Drug could win.

I heard two nominees discussing the selection process in loud whispers, as if they wanted me to overhear.

"It's not fair!" declared Julie Jensen, a tall brunette and daughter of the milk trucker. "Her mother is a Williamson, so she's related to half the town. She could actually win! Look at that awful hairdo! And that flat chest—well, it was flat last week. I'll bet she's wearing falsies. Wouldn't that be awful—having her represent the town in every parade throughout Polk County for an entire year!"

"They ought to have a real beauty competition, with swimsuits and all," a buxom blonde named Connie Lynch agreed. "This system really is a farce."

I tossed my head, silently counting my assets: deep blue eyes with finely arched brows, high cheekbones, clear skin, straight teeth, and a good smile. I was five foot three and slim—a perfect size seven. I had borrowed a size-nine party dress from my friend Louise and basted it with temporary tucks around the waist and bodice. After I had stuffed my bra with nylon stockings, it was a fairly decent fit.

A pair of wrist-length gloves concealed my bitten fingernails, still ragged and stubby after years of struggle with my shameful habit. I was also handicapped by fine, unruly hair. I had not asked for Mama's help—not at this busy time of year. Besides, she would only have replied, as usual, that she couldn't understand why I fretted so about my appearance.

"You have good straight posture. You look strong and healthy." That was her highest compliment.

She said as much about her Holstein heifers. I needed much more bolstering than that. When I pressed her, Mama added, "Well, you're lucky—you've had first-rate dental care and sensible shoes. That counts for something. Teeth have to last a lifetime. And bunions or fallen arches always show around the eyes and mouth."

Mama would never encourage me, nor any of her daughters, to aim for beauty. She said it was a waste of time, a selfish, shallow goal that led to disappointment and despair.

I was not sure that Daddy agreed. He never contradicted Mama, but he often raised an eyebrow or grinned crookedly whenever I looked especially nice. And he seemed pleased by my involvement in the Sweet Corn Festival.

"No contest," Daddy had chuckled. "You'll win for sure—you might as well start practicing that wave they do, right now." He pulled a greasy cotton work glove over his right hand and twisted it from side to side in perfect imitation of a Milltown queen.

"The wave is easy, Daddy! It's this awful head of hair that worries me."

"I think your hair looks fine. But I'll be glad to help you out if you want to try the beauty shop in town."

"No, thanks, Daddy. I'll figure something out myself."

I had saved the money and had almost scheduled an appointment. But when I passed by Dorothy's Beauty Parlor, the chemical fumes curling through the open door smelled foreign and forbidding. The elaborate French twists and teased-up styles displayed in Dorothy's window were for Milltown matrons, not for country girls like me.

I trimmed and bobby-pinned my hair and prayed for low humidity on pageant day. God answered me with muggy heat, ninety-eight degrees on the makeshift stage erected next to Miller Hardware. It was a curl-wilting, mascara-melting afternoon. Dressed in a borrowed sheath of pale green taffeta, I felt like a cob of sweet corn swelling in the husk. I knew my rivals must be roasting, too. When Julie Jensen—the princess with the spiteful tongue—was pronounced Miss Congeniality, she could barely smile.

I heard my name. Gail Johnston, the outgoing queen, stepped forward and placed her rhinestone crown upon my head. John Dann, the mayor, laid a dozen long-stemmed roses in my arms. They led me down the steps and across the shimmering blacktop to the deck of a white Impala convertible upholstered in blue leather.

I felt elated as the parade moved forward. This might be a silly, small-town festival, but it sang with energy and color. Midway through town our car stopped for the photographers. A loudspeaker blared my name, and we glided forward—three blocks down Main Street, three blocks back. I forgot the wagonload of

Sara (left), Susie, and escorts at the Junior Prom, Unity High School, May 1960

sullen beauties behind me. I barely heard the high school band play "March Triumphant," scarcely saw the team of Belgian horses, the 4-H floats and homespun clowns and kiddie cars weaving figure-eights across the street. I saw my family—all six Helleruds and several aunts and uncles—in front of Lindoo Drug, waving excitedly. There was practical Mama, always so concerned about my teeth and arches. She was busy with her Kodak, trying to capture all the pageantry. Daddy was laughing, touching the visor of his bright, green cap in a seedcorn salute.

I forgot about my spoiled hair, my plumped-up bodice, and my stubby fingernails. I didn't wonder at my coronation or worry how it came to be. I waved at my proud public, and I felt like royalty.

Sweet Corn Queen. At sixteen I was a monarch. I felt adorable—and equal with my talented twin sister. Superior, even, in all the ways that mattered to a teenaged girl. I spent my car-hop tips on makeup and a cashmere sweater, which I refused to share with Susie. She wouldn't care, I knew, because she sometimes wore the same mismatched outfit two or three days running. Besides, I couldn't loan my cashmere to someone who was always losing buttons or coming home all snagged and gravy stained. That fall the football stars and basketball heroes began phoning me for dates. I said yes, of course, I'd be delighted. Yes, yes, to everyone who called, even when I wasn't sure I liked or trusted them. Sometimes I almost wanted Mama or Daddy to say no, I couldn't go so often, and not with boys from neighboring towns, boys I hardly knew at all.

They tried to rein me in a little. Usually they wavered, exchanging wary glances, acting proud and anxious and confused about my sudden popularity. Peggy had been so painfully ignored all through her teens. This situation must have been a welcome—if perplexing—challenge.

Did I really need to go out two or three nights every week? Who were these boys who called? Were they good students? What were their parents' names? Their grandparents? Were they Scandinavian? Farmers? Lutherans? Had they lived long in the area? Did they keep a tidy house and pay their bills? I tried to answer all their silly questions, even when they pried too deep for comfort.

"What do you kids find to do till midnight," Mama asked,

"when Main Street is shut down tight and decent folks are sound asleep in bed?"

"We drive around. And talk," I said, defensively.

"All that gas, to run around in circles! How wasteful!"

"Well, you be home by ten-thirty on week nights and midnight on the weekends," Daddy warned.

"We've taught you proper manners and sound values, so we shouldn't have to worry, should we?" Mama added, clearly wanting reassurance.

"No, you shouldn't," I agreed.

But dating was a tricky business. I knew well how to please and charm; yet I felt scared and vulnerable. Everything was flying out of balance. Worst of all, my twin was acting hurt and jealous.

"Who's taking you out tonight?" Susie wondered. "And where will you be going?"

"It's only Jimmy Larson," I told her. "It's hard to get excited about someone you've known since first grade, even if he did make two touchdowns in the homecoming game. We'll probably get a hamburger at the Mill Inn or go to the drive-in movie. Or just drive around town in that beat-up car of his. You're not missing much."

I didn't tell her about the long hours of parking on dead-end roads, the urgent kissing, the petting and probing I both dreaded and craved. I wouldn't tell about his steamy breath that fogged the windows of the '52 Chevy, erasing the starlight, trapping me inside. I wouldn't tell her that I sometimes had to beg and plead to be delivered safely home.

But I had always made it so far. Innocence intact. It was a thrilling caper, both fun and frightening. I was dancing on ledges, pirouetting, learning the power of my newfound beauty, testing the borders of a chasm so compelling that I felt I must be doomed to fall.

❧ The Capping ❧

A month after I became the Milltown Sweet Corn Queen, Peggy won her own bright crown—the nursing cap awarded by Swedish Hospital School of Nursing in Minneapolis.

Six eager Helleruds attended the capping ceremony at First Covenant Church. It began impressively with two columns of student nurses in starched white uniforms marching up the center aisle, bearing lighted candles in their outstretched hands. They formed a chorus before the altar and chanted the Florence Nightingale pledge:

> I solemnly pledge myself before God in the presence of this assembly to pass my life in purity and to practice my profession faithfully. I will abstain from whatever is deleterious and mischievous and will not take or knowingly administer any harmful drug.

Peggy should be allowed to skip the pledge, I said to myself. God made her so earnest and pure. She's never had a mischievous motive in her life.

Mama and Daddy sat forward in the pew, rigid with pride. I wondered if they were recalling Peggy's long obsession with nursing, which began when she was seven and in bed with pneumonia. I remembered well—although I was only four—Peggy's fever and delirium. She saw imaginary worms and spiders on the walls, but it was not the insects that revolted her. It was the sight of her twin sisters lurking at the bedroom door.

"I hate those twins! They make me sick! Just keep them out of here!"

Susie and I cowered in the hallway, feeling despised and horribly responsible, praying for our sister's recovery.

Mama said it was not our fault at all and explained why Peggy was so ill. She had talked out of turn in her second-grade classroom. Miss Paulson, who believed in firm, swift discipline, kept Peggy fifteen minutes after school, dusting erasers and cleaning blackboards. The school bus could not wait. There was no telephone at home, no way to call for transportation. Peggy walked two miles home from school in windy subzero weather and caught a terrible chill. The next morning she was burning up with fever. Dr. Hoff diagnosed pneumonia in both lungs. It would be dangerous, he said, to try to move her to Amery Hospital, fifteen miles away. He would make house calls every day and keep an eye on her condition.

It was a hard winter with record snowfalls. Daddy kept the walk shoveled, the driveway plowed and ready for Dr. Hoff's visits. Every morning we watched for the hopeful shape of his dark blue Ford sedan moving up the driveway, barely visible above the ragged banks of snow. Susie and I waited anxiously in the doorway while the doctor put his stethoscope to Peggy's chest, fed her pills from his black bag, and sponged her limbs with alcohol. Finally one afternoon her fever broke and the bugs and worms crawled down off the walls, leaving only the comfortably faded wallpaper roses.

> I will do all in my power to maintain and elevate the standard of my profession and will hold in confidence all personal matters committed to my keeping and all family affairs coming to my knowledge in the practice of my calling.

Daddy bought Peggy a thick, spiral-bound scrapbook to occupy her during the long days in bed. Soon she was clipping pictures of nurses and doctors and hypodermic needles from the meager selection of magazines our household had to offer. The scrapbook bulged once she decided to include real stuff—dried scabs and bloodied bandages and globs of reddish-brown wax scooped out of her reluctant sisters' ear canals.

Our family was a fairly healthy lot, discounting a few unlucky accidents. Common complaints were easily handled by enemas or steam tents or a cheesecloth bag of sliced onions tied round the neck at bedtime. That was Mama's favorite cure for chest colds and stuffy sinuses, and it seemed to work miracles. Most of us were anxious to avoid the onion cure, so we seldom reported any respiratory symptoms. However, Susie chewed the corners of her bag and grew to like the taste of onions, half-cooked against her fevered chest. "Ugh! You're eating those stinky things?" I asked, thoroughly revolted. "Well, they're kind of sweet," she answered.

Sturdy and uncomplaining as we were, Peggy often had to wait a long time for her scrapbook specimens. The cows and sheep came down with fascinating ailments—scours, hoof-scald, and caked udders—but Peggy was particular about what went into her scrapbook. Nothing less than human tissue—or human secretions—would do.

"Isn't it about time somebody got hurt or sick around here?" Peggy asked impatiently. "How am I ever going to learn about nursing this way?" It seemed to me she was involved in a troubling conflict—praying each night for our continued health and happiness, yet wishing illness and injury upon us all.

Fragments of the cast from Susie's broken leg were preserved in the scrapbook. Susie obliged her again in the spring of 1950 by tumbling out of an apple tree, ripping a gash in her upper left arm. Peggy inspected the wound and found it deep and gaping, with yellow fatty tissue bursting through.

"It's going to need stitches," she declared. "I'm coming with you."

Daddy drove, and Peggy tagged along to the doctor's office in Balsam Lake. She watched the stitching with fascination and also collected seven shriveled knots of catgut when they were snipped from Susie's healing wound the following week. Into the scrapbook they went, framed with cellophane and adhesive tape, labeled carefully for future inspiration.

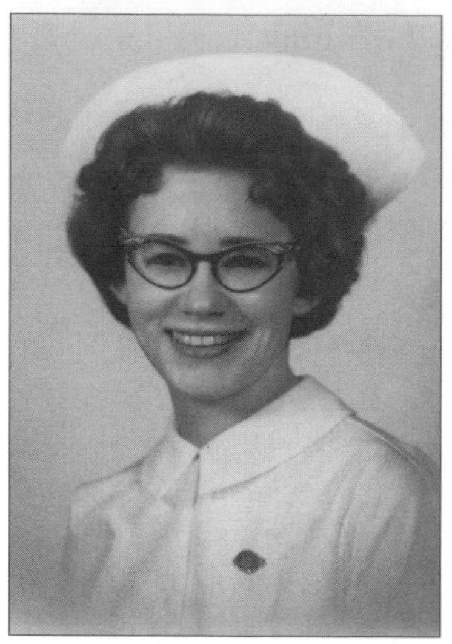

Margaret Ann Hellerud, graduate nurse, 1961

My sisters and I were all plagued with tonsillitis in the early 1950s. In one expensive season all the poisoned organs were surgically removed. Susie and I suffered loudly and miserably from the procedure. Peggy, who had high tolerance for pain, did not complain. She felt well rewarded by a laboratory of little glass bottles containing three pairs of purply-brown organs suspended in formaldehyde.

I looked at Daddy, sitting on the edge of his pew. I guessed he might be thinking about the day Peggy left for nursing school on the Greyhound bus. He had meant to drive her to Minneapolis, help her get settled and all, but there were twenty acres of second-crop hay lying cut in the fields and thunderclouds rolling in from the west. Peggy had gripped those suitcases as if they contained the crown jewels instead of her home-sewed wardrobe and a few new pairs of underpants from the Milltown Co-op. She was struggling for composure.

"You take this extra cash and don't worry about the cab fare, no matter what it costs. The driver will take you right to your door." Daddy said it over and over, as if he was plenty uncomfortable about trusting his daughter to a city stranger.

It rained all right, three or four inches, right after the last of the hay was gathered in. But Daddy did not seem too pleased.

"Damn the hay! I should have let it rot. I should never have sent her off on the bus, all alone like that."

"But she called us from the dormitory, Harvey. She made it on her own, just fine."

Mama's reassurance didn't help. He should have driven her to Minneapolis. He had wanted to go with her. He might at least have spared her some anxiety and eased the wrenching separation for his daughter, for himself.

"It's wrong. It's crazy, when a fellow lets a goddamn field of hay stand in the way of something so important. . . . I should never have sent her off alone . . . "

He would say it several times over the years. It was one of those great regrets that he had to live with, an aching omission that could never be corrected or forgiven.

> With loyalty I will endeavor to aid the physician in his work, and devote myself to the welfare of those committed to my care.

The student nurses faced the congregation. One by one their names were called.

Margaret Ann Hellerud. My sister stepped forward and bowed her head as she received the cap, stiff and white as a little sail borne on a freshened breeze.

Grandpa Hellerud

A few days after Grandpa Hellerud's death, Daddy received a letter from the manager of the Roseland Hotel in Portland, Oregon, where Grandpa had been living on and off for several years. The manager expressed his deep regrets that Henry Hellerud had suffered a heart attack and died alone in his hotel room. He added that Mr. Hellerud had been tidy and circumspect in personal habits and demeanor—a model guest in every way.

Polk County Ledger
Balsam Lake, Wisconsin
September 19, 1963

Henry J. Hellerud was born March 17, 1887, at Halstad, Minnesota, the oldest son of Nellie and Bertram Hellerud. He was baptized and confirmed in the Anthony Lutheran Church. He attended Concordia College at Moorhead, Minnesota, and taught school near his home. The school ground was originally part of the Hellerud farm, and had been given to the district by his father.

Later he studied railroad telegraphy in Minneapolis. He was the station agent at Milltown from 1909 to 1953, except for two years at Trenary, Michigan, and Thief River Falls, Minnesota. On June 3, 1910, he married Agnes Christensen of Milltown, who preceded him in death in 1947.

Surviving are a daughter, Wanda (Mrs. John Ostrom), Lindstrom, Minnesota, and a son Harvey, of Milltown, eight grandchildren and two great grandchildren, four brothers, Theodore, Carl, Martin, and Alfred Hellerud, and one sister, (Mrs. George Sulerud), of Halstad. One brother, Bennett, was killed in action in France during World War I.

The forty-four years that Mr. Hellerud served as station agent were the busiest in railroad transportation. Those who remember Milltown thru two world wars will also recall that for many years the area was served daily by 4 passenger trains, 2 night passengers, 2 way freights, and several extras. The number of telegrams received and sent from his station is beyond calculation. He sent innumerable emergency telegrams any hour of the night when asked, as well as those during the day. During many of these years, a telephone was a luxury, and after hours he delivered personally countless telegrams to people in the resort areas and on the farms. . . .

The depot was at first located where the cannery now stands. Later, when it was moved and enlarged, Mr. Hellerud laid the side-walk from the depot to the main street crossing at his own expense. In those days, each evening the station agent lit the kerosene-burning switch lights and also the semaphore light high above the depot.

There were many interesting experiences in early railroading. On one occasion, about 1913, the passenger train was stuck in the snow for three days in the cut near the present site of the cannery. On stock shipping days there was extra activity. The stock yards were located where the feed mill now stands and waiting rigs were lined up from the yards to the main crossing. At one time during a severe storm, Mr. Hellerud caught a runaway freight car, climbed to the top, and set the brakes. On another occasion, he saw the southbound afternoon flier jump the track in front of the depot, and watched it miraculously jump back on the track again without incident.

After his retirement, Mr. Hellerud divided his time between Minneapolis and Portland. He passed away in his hotel room September 6 following a heart attack.

Unfortunately, no one at the Roseland had been closely acquainted with Mr. Hellerud; no doubt they had missed knowing a fine gentleman.

"What a thoughtful letter," Mama said.

Daddy shook his head. "He lived the better part of four or five years at the Roseland. And nobody knew him. Well, that figures."

I thought about my own fleeting contacts with this strangely distant Grandpa. Throughout my childhood, he made occasional visits to the farm. He arrived dressed in his railroad jacket with gold Soo Line buttons or in a natty three-piece suit. His polished wing-tip shoes were unfit for tramping through the woods or visiting a litter of new kittens in the barn. He pushed his wire-rimmed glasses tight against the bridge of his fine nose, smoothed his sparse white hair, and checked his pocket watch repeatedly, as if waiting for an outbound train. He was always brisk and cordial, laughing politely with his shoulders, never with his eyes. He didn't touch us, didn't talk a lot except to comment on the weather or the fact that Daddy didn't take a daily paper and a person could get quickly out of touch with markets and politics that way. A model guest, he praised the food, hung his hand towel neatly on the rod, and never overstayed.

I had already moved away from home when Henry Hellerud died in 1963. I returned home for the funeral and stayed awhile.

I was not grieving deeply. None of the grandkids seemed to feel a great loss. We were glad to learn that Grandpa had been quite a savvy investor. Daddy's share of the inheritance was enough to dig a better well, modernize the house, build a double corn crib, and erect a concrete silo. All those overdue improvements should have cheered Daddy, but he seemed tense and tired. The day of Grandpa's funeral he began shaking with hiccoughs. The spasms continued for days, until his ribs ached and he grew weak from loss of sleep and appetite. He took great gulps of water, breathed into paper bags, swallowed spoonfuls of thick honey. Nothing worked. Finally he saw the doctor, but strong sedation offered only temporary respite.

My throat hurt for him; my chest felt tight and sore. One

evening as I helped Daddy feed the calves he asked if I remembered Grandpa's sudden, brief visits to the farm after he had retired and moved to Minneapolis.

I remembered, all right. Grandpa's timing was terrible. He always called at chore time from some depot twenty miles down the line. Daddy would have to leave Mama in charge of the milking and drive an hour or more round trip when Grandpa could just as well have taken the train all the way to Milltown.

"Maybe he was afraid he would feel sad coming into that depot where he worked so many years," I offered.

"Nah," said Daddy. "He was just afraid he'd have to make some small talk or that someone might want to know his business. I'll never understand why he was so darned shy and afraid to let people get to know him—as if they were out to hurt him, as if he had something to hide. And after forty years in a community where he was so respected! Well, I'm done driving all over the countryside to pick him up at Soo Line stations. I had that coffin shipped straight to the Milltown depot."

He said all that without a spasm.

The next day Daddy and I visited Grandpa Hellerud's grave in the Milltown cemetery. He had been buried beside his wife, Agnes. The large, granite headstone had not yet been inscribed with Grandpa's year of death. It was a handsome marker:

Hellerud

Henry J.	Agnes F.
1887–	1882–1947

"He wanted me to farm, you see. Said that way I could always feed my kids, and a farm would keep me out of war. He'd worked the telegraph through World War I and delivered enough bad news to families whose sons were killed or missing in action overseas. But damn! I was no farmer! He wouldn't listen—just insisted he knew best."

He said all that, despite an attack of hiccoughs. It seemed as if all the words Grandpa and Daddy never spoke were wadded up, convulsing in his throat.

"Those were tough times, Depression years. But Dad had it good with the railroad. My sister Wanda got a college education, and I got a small down payment on a piece of rocky ground. Well, by God, I did my battle with that land. I picked rocks and plowed and fertilized till I was ready to drop. I cut hay and grew corn and put up tons of silage and threshed oats and farmed that pitiful soil as well as any man could possibly do. I don't know how or why, but I hung tough all those years, and he couldn't manage one word of encouragement or praise, not one word, not ever . . . "

Daddy was shaking his clenched fist at Grandpa's tombstone, no longer addressing me. I moved away and studied the neighboring markers. Daddy stood in place, explaining, pleading, weeping for what seemed like a long time.

At dusk we walked back to the car and drove home in easy silence. When Daddy turned off the ignition, I realized that his hiccoughs had been left behind.

Grandpa Hellerud gave me more than I once imagined. It took me a couple of decades to know it. Although he did not share his thoughts and feelings, he held out something large and lasting—a taste of railroading when it was flavored with magic and might.

He gave me a long, low, wooden depot, mustard color, trimmed in brown, skirted by concrete ramps and docks, positioned on the east end of Milltown parallel to the Soo Line rails. He gave me endless miles of track. He furnished pennies for the gum machine mounted on the wainscoted wall of the passenger lounge. I placed my penny in the slot, heard it drop, and cupped my hands beneath the chute, collecting a miniature yellow carton that held two sugar-coated pellets of Chiclets gum. I chewed on travel and adventure.

He allowed me to kneel on the ties and place my ear against the track five minutes before train time so I could hear the three-o-nine singing down the line, all the way from Centuria. When it rumbled like a bass drum, when the rail began to tremble in my hands, he called me back. The danger pulsed down through my body, holding me one dreadful second longer, then released me in a breathless resurrection.

Occasionally Grandpa Hellerud punched out three cardboard tickets, suggesting my sisters and I ride up the line to the village of Luck and back. We settled into the plush, velvet seats and strained to hear the conversations of our fellow passengers, wondering what their important missions might be. One Sunday afternoon we heard the idle remarks of a finely dressed couple seated directly behind us.

"Whatever is the purpose of all these tiny towns along the way? Do you suppose that every single village has a name?"

"Of course they do—the names are painted on the railroad depots. I can't imagine living way out here, can you?"

The fields of tasseling corn flew by. Red barns, brick silos, houses ringed with oak and elm passed like transient outposts, poorly rooted in the landscape. These homesteads were not grand enough to claim all your time and energy, your very life. And yet they did; they did.

Things looked so different from the window of a speeding train. We were disturbed to realize the world was so vast, to know a farm was such a fleeting thing. Even Milltown was so small, so insignificant that it was scarcely worthy of a name.

"How was your trip?" Grandpa asked absently when we returned on the southbound run at 4:05.

"Just fine."

We could not share our rich impressions. Grandpa was not fond of conversation. Nor did he offer hugs or smiles or birthday presents. He made a brief whistle-stop each Christmas, delivering his predictable gifts—large, two-layered boxes of chocolate-covered cherries. We were never surprised, but always pleased. Seven boxes, one for each. Something we didn't have to share.

Susie ate hers greedily, several candies every day, and they were gone before the New Year. I rewarded myself sparingly, trying to make the candy last till Easter. Carefully selecting the moment, I nipped a hole in the casing, sucked the sweet syrup, chewed and swallowed the tart cherry in tiny bites, and savored the rich, smooth chocolate that coated my teeth and tongue.

The chocolates kept coming, year after year, even after Grandpa retired from the Soo Line and moved to an apartment in the city where he could live in solitude at last. They came by parcel post from Minneapolis, then from Portland, until Grandpa was gone.

I buy my own chocolate-covered cherries now, and they taste of Henry Hellerud. I know his essence after all these years.

He is a weathered railroad station in a pioneer village. He is a blackened wood stove in the center of the waiting room. He is stout oak benches set in lacy metal frames where the passengers sit, nervously waiting for their trains to pull in. He is the ticking of a Regulator clock, the tapping of a coded message across a wire to a distant place.

He is a sturdy Smith-Corona, sometimes with clacking keys, more often hooded and silent. He is a rack of rubber stamps, a bill of lading. He is mail bags heaved onto boxcars, parcels tossed down to the loading dock. He smells of pungent creosote, of steam and coal and fire.

He is the silver locomotive barely visible in the distance, looming into view, threatening to swallow me within its massive steaming wheels. The train passes, shrieking, then grinding and stopping, waiting, wheezing again, lurching, churning forward, sucking juice from iron, curling through the hillsides with a melancholy sigh.

Pomp and Circumstances

March 18, 1961

Dear Mugsy,

Ours has been a busy house this winter, and things are not slowing down with Susan and Sara graduating from the new Unity High School (Milltown, Balsam Lake, and Centuria consolidated) in just two months. Susan's music accounts for most of her activities. She has had a couple of boyfriends on the string this winter and it seems that one of them has finally gotten jealous of her piano, so I guess he is out of the picture for the time being. Talking of eloping saving parents a lot of trouble and expense, Ron said—just in fun of course—"No danger you'll ever elope, Susie." "Why not?" says she. "You could never manage to get your piano down the ladder." She said she managed to take it good naturedly, but he meant it just the same and it sort of riled her.

Wonder if he will still feel the same about the piano when he hears the latest: Susan won the Thursday Musical award in piano last Thursday—and another $100 scholarship. (Program enclosed.)

Sara went down with her. Peggy and her roommate attended also. The kids all piled into a phone booth and called me after they finished their lunch at the YMCA. I know this competition is keen and the kids feel honored to be in the finals, even without winning. Only one prize is given in each division. The flutist won first in instrumental this year; there were no vocalists. Sara said she went up to congratulate the flutist, who said to Sara, "How in the world did you change clothes so fast?" She thought it was Susan, of course. Mrs. Hiner, Susan's teacher, made the same mistake, so Sara spent most of her time straightening people out. She got a kick out of that. Strange the boyfriends never get them mixed up!

Peggy will be graduating from nursing school on August 20th and will have two weeks vacation, before continuing her degree program at the University of Wisconsin. She may be eligible for a federal grant of $200 per month. She has paid her own way so far and done a mighty good job.

I'll have to keep this short—will try to write again soon.

Hope all is well with you. We're already counting the days until your summer visit!

Love,

Helen and Family

Unity School District
Polk County, Wisconsin
Milltown, Wisconsin

May 16, 1961

Mr. & Mrs. Harvey Hellerud
Milltown, Wisconsin
Dear Mr. & Mrs. Hellerud:

It gives me great pleasure to write this letter to you congratulating you and your daughters Sara and Susan for their accomplishments while attending high school. The main objective of our teachers is to assist each student as an individual and to enable him to have a good sound basic understanding from which to work. We are sure that your daughters have worked hard to achieve their scholastic aver-

ages, which was 3.856 for Sara and 3.919 for Susan, in their four years in high school placing them on the honor roll. In addition to their scholastic work Sara and Susan have taken an active part in other school activities. Sara participated in FHA, Pep Club, Tumbling, Chorus, Band, All Star Band, Pep Band, Eagle's Eye Staff, Student Council, Class Play, One Act Plays and Forensics Club. Susan in FHA, Chorus, Band, All Star Band, Eagle's Eye Staff, Class Play, One Act Plays, French Club, State solo, and Forensics Club.

Once again I would like to congratulate you for giving us this opportunity to work with them, it has been a pleasure for both the teachers and the administration to have girls like these in our school. Thank you.

Sincerely yours,

Neil L. Binkley, Superintendent

Neil Binkley, our high school superintendent, was a tall, impressive man and a skilled orator. On May 18, 1961, he addressed the senior class of Unity High School, Milltown, Wisconsin. It was a touching tribute to "Our Cherished Years." We graduates had learned our lessons well, he said. We were schooled in history, geography, chemistry, mathematics, English composition, and much more. We knew the importance of teamwork, sportsmanship, and integrity, but we had a few things yet to discover. One of those discoveries would be appreciation of the cherished years that lay behind us. We had been loved and protected, supported by teachers, family, and friends. Life would never be so easy or so safe again.

It was hard for me to take him seriously. Two years earlier Daddy had caught him stealing sheep manure from an abandoned shed in our northeast pasture. Both men had been embarrassed. Daddy had sent him off with one small gunnysack of fertilizer—barely enough to fortify his roses one brief season. Daddy had reported this at suppertime, with a mixture of amusement and disdain.

"If the man had only asked, I would gladly have filled all his sacks and promised him a lifetime supply."

Now, as I heard Mr. Binkley's sentimental message I thought: Sheep manure! These have been the best years of my life? These memories should be cherished forever? Yes, I've had a few proud moments, but don't tell me that it's all downhill from here. If this is as good as it ever gets, I don't think I want to live.

I thought about my lousy start—first grade in Balsam Lake—with Miss Paulson ordering all heads down on the desks, touring up and down the aisles, making her inspections. Most of the shiny blonde heads got nothing but a casual glance. The black-haired Indian kids were subjected to a rigorous review. And because Susie and I enjoyed playing with two Indian girls, who had a lively last name—Wakemeup—which matched their personalities, our stringy locks were suspect, too. Miss Paulson parted clumps of hair with her fingernails and raked her long digits through the fine strands at the back of our burning necks. We squirmed with shame and dread.

"Here's a big fellow!" she announced with glee. "Oh, my, a whole nest of nits here!"

Then Susie and I and our Chippewa playmates would be culled out and driven home in disgrace.

We knew the routine: we headed straight to the sheep shed where Daddy would douse our heads with the same stout insecticide he used to rid the sheep of ticks and vermin. It burned the scalp and made stiff thatches of our fine, straight hair, but we knew better than to object or complain. The stuff worked. Within twenty-four hours we would be back in school, louse free and ready for Miss Paulson's meticulous review.

After Mama warned us not to share our hats or combs, the infestations ceased.

Soon after we got the head lice under control, a family of skunks moved into the crawl space beneath our kitchen floor. Peggy, Susie, and I annoyed these temperamental creatures on an April morning as we tromped around the kitchen getting ready for school. The skunks sent up a powerful protest. Their stench permeated our hair and clothing and followed us onto the school bus and into the classroom.

Our schoolmates were unkind. "*Pee-yew! I smell skunk!*" They held their noses, sneering in our general direction, careful not to come too close.

We endured the taunts and insults all day long. That night we bathed in Fels Naptha. Mama scrubbed our clothes and washed the kitchen down with Lysol, even sponged the oilcloth covers on our books.

We tiptoed through the house for weeks, hoping to placate the high-strung rodents nesting beneath our feet. They released samples of their ghastly perfume now and then, just to remind us who was in control. They would have peace and quiet now and move along when they were ready, not before.

It seemed to take forever, but at last the young skunks grew to adolescence and demanded freedom. The entire family emerged from the foundation on a summer day and ambled into the woods. We Helleruds would not be liberated quite so easily. We were cruelly labeled "the Smellerud kids" for years to come.

My sisters and I were glad to leave this ridicule behind when we moved to Milltown in the fall of 1953. But fresh miseries awaited. Nearly all of our new classmates had television sets at home. They chattered every lunch and recess about their favorite shows—*Superman, Roy Rogers, I Love Lucy*. We felt miserably excluded. We begged and pleaded for a television set, but Mama and Daddy had no intention of buying a "one-eyed monster" for our home. It was passive entertainment, Mama said, and we didn't have the time to watch it anyway.

"It's not that we can't afford it," Mama explained time and time again. "It's just that we have more important places for our money. And besides your father and I don't *believe* in television."

Didn't *believe* in it! There it stood, big as life, in every living room in Polk County.

To prove their point, our parents bought an expensive set of reference books. This would stimulate our minds more than the Mouseketeers or Hopalong Cassidy could ever hope to do. We thumbed through the silent pages in despair. Did they think we could impress our friends by spouting facts from eighteen volumes of the *Encyclopaedia Britannica?*

When we finally understood that Mama and Daddy planned to raise us to adulthood without the benefit of television, we begged them at least to erect an aerial on the roof. They refused. So the absence of a TV antenna atop our house announced to all the school-bus riders—all the passing world—that we were sadly disadvantaged.

Our social image suffered further during early adolescence. Increasingly absorbed with her music, Susie did not worry over her appearance, but I agonized enough for both of us. My weary hand-me-down crinolines were never stiff enough. My full skirts were not full enough, the sheath skirts were not tight enough. I wore thin anklets and yearned for bulky bobby-sox. My straight, stubborn hair, while free of lice, was never right, despite tortured nights with a headful of bristly brush-and-metal rollers. I wore sturdy oxfords or saddle shoes when penny loafers were in vogue.

"Your arches will fall if I let you wear those floppy shoes!"

Mama shrieked. "Would you like to be flat-footed for the rest of your life for the sake of fashion?"

You bet I would.

"You let Peggy wear loafers. What makes her so different?" I persisted.

"Well, she's older—anyway, I shouldn't have to explain that to you," Mama said defensively. She knew it weakened her position. She finally relented and bought the loafers "just for special occasions," but by then my classmates had discovered tennis shoes and nylon stockings.

"Canvas shoes and silk socks in January!" Mama snorted. "Over my dead body! Remember how we almost lost Peggy back in 1947? No kid of mine will ever again come down with pneumonia for lack of proper clothing!"

I cringed at the way she said "silk socks," as if it were still World War II and nylon hadn't been invented.

Even worse, she made us all tog up in bulky home-knit mittens and three-cornered woolen scarves, like a troop of Russian peasants. The quicker we lost the dreaded mittens or unraveled the thumbs, the faster her knitting needles flew, cranking out an inexhaustible supply. The woman was a tyrant and a sorceress.

Our ugly, zippered stadium boots were the final insult—usually a size too large so they could "serve an extra season." Town kids did not dress like that. We had no choice but to remove some winter gear and stash it in the culvert before the school bus loomed in view. Then we would tiptoe over the snowbank and stuff our freezing hands into our pockets, defying wind and sleet and numbing cold. Once we carelessly tossed our scarves and boots and mittens into the bare branches of a lilac bush. Daddy found the cache of clothing when he went out to fetch the mail, and there was hell to pay.

It wasn't "cool" to be so warmly dressed. Why couldn't they understand?

Senior class pictures, 1961, Susan Marie Hellerud, left, and Sara Jane Hellerud, right

They never learned.

Yet Susie and I weathered the humiliations imposed by parents who worried for our welfare and loved us too dearly for comfort.

Here we stood, on May 18, 1961, fully grown, graduating from high school. We would soon go trailing off like those young skunks. We were about to leave the cherished years behind and learn some lessons from the wider world.

Setting Sail

Excerpt from Sara's Journal
Saturday, May 13, 1961

After two days in bed with a terrible cold, I was finally well enough to go back to school Thursday morning. Thank God! Because we had the dress rehearsal for our Senior Class Play that night—Thornton Wilder's Our Town. We rehearsed until 11:00 P.M. Aunty Adele is a wonderful director! The play should be the best this town has ever seen.

We didn't have a single class on Friday, since we were busy with graduation practice, working on the play, etc. We gave a matinee for the high school kids Friday afternoon. It was even more stirring than I had imagined it would be. Or was it just us? During the death scene, several of us occupying the "graves" in the cemetery found that tears were coursing down our cheeks. I will never forget how it felt—one of the richest experiences of my high school days. I nearly sobbed out loud, which would not have a been good thing for a corpse to do. When the play was over, we actors rushed to the dressing room and had a good hugging and crying session.

I'm not sure if all this emotion was due to Wilder's powerful play, or simply the fact that our high school days are nearly over. These past four years have been wonderful, terrifying, rewarding, difficult, exciting and horrible, all at the same time. But the most painful part of this ending is saying good-bye to all these super friends.

Our public performance was scheduled for Friday evening, and we were all set to begin at 8:15, when a thun-

derstorm broke loose and—darkness! Power failure! After two hours we were still without any lights, and the play had to be called off. It was rescheduled for next Tuesday night. Disappointing, but during the long wait, Mama entertained the audience on the piano, and before long there was a regular "community sing" going on. When everyone joined in "The Halls of Ivy," I sat on the back bleachers and cried. I just never thought graduation would affect me this way.

Monday, May 15, 1961

I don't know just why I'm feeling so dejected. It has nothing to do with my birthday—or non-birthday, rather. Susie and I are used to that after all these years. It's no one's fault—just plain bad luck—that we were born at planting time when everyone is so terribly busy.

Well, I am eighteen years old now, but I don't feel any different. I should be quite a grown-up young lady now. But I'm afraid I am almost as childish and immature as I was at thirteen. Susie seems older. Maybe her music has helped her get beyond herself somehow. Oh, Mama, Mama! I'm just a little girl, not eighteen and ready to leave home. I will have to do a great deal of growing up this summer.

Mama, I do love you so much—more than anyone else in this world, I think. I would die for you. Why am I so unwilling to sacrifice some of my selfish pleasures to help you more? Or even to improve my disposition and make your life a little more pleasant? I am just like Emily in Our Town—young and blind and ignorant, shut up in my own little box. Tomorrow morning I will probably forget about all this, and once again "go up and down, trampling on the feelings of those about me."

It's 1:00 A.M. *Goodnight, dear Mama, Daddy, Susie, Teddy, Peggy, Priscilla. Goodnight, dear, lonely Aunty Adele, Grandma and Papa, and all the dear ones in the world who love me in spite of my moodiness and selfishness. I will try to do better tomorrow.*

Mama aimed her camera toward the sheep shed one last time before we lost it in the autumn storm of 1962. The structure tilts precariously. Its window frames are vacant eyes, staring out upon a silent meadow. The sheep are gone. A large pointed object protrudes from the south entrance of the shed: it is the bowsprit of a sailboat.

The fall of 1961 my twin and I prepared to separate—she to study music in Minneapolis and I to the University of Wisconsin campus in nearby Eau Claire. Dividing our wardrobe and personal possessions was an agonizing task.

"You take that Pendleton skirt and matching blazer," I told Susie. "You'll need them."

"No, Sara, it always looked better on you. Besides, musicians are supposed to be poor, you know, kind of Bohemian. You never see them wearing that kind of thing. It will be perfect at the university campus."

For eighteen years we had shared everything. Now, instead of fighting for the valuables, we urged them on one another, hoping material sacrifice might somehow ease the loss.

Daddy seemed to be planning another kind of departure, but none of us talked about it much. He had relinquished many responsibilities to Teddy, who at fifteen was good at field work and a clever mechanic. Mama managed the dairy herd. Mother and son made an efficient team. Daddy was functioning like a hired hand, quietly taking directions from both of them, but his years of labor and frustration had earned him some spare time and special privileges. He had always enjoyed carpentry, building sleds, toboggans, and birdhouses over the years, always with painstaking care. But his latest project was more ambitious; he was spending hours each day constructing a sailboat in an abandoned sheep shed.

The boat was large; the twenty-eight-foot sailing vessel nearly filled the building. As far as we knew, our father had never stepped aboard a sailboat in his life. Yet he was consulting no sailors, no shipbuilders, and had nothing but his own rough sketches to guide him. He purchased truckloads of material from the local lumberyard, deflecting or ignoring all questions about his plans and purposes. Patiently he planed and sawed and glued and clamped, until a graceful sailing sloop appeared upon the sea of dried sheep manure.

And where would he be launching this outsized craft? Surely not on Half Moon Lake, already crowded with pontoons and motorboats.

Mama did not comment much or pester Daddy when he was busy in his shipyard.

"How will he ever get it out, Mama?" my sisters and I worried. "It's way too big to get through either door."

"That old shed . . . what does it matter?" she shrugged. "I expect he'll pull the shed down when he's ready."

The boat was nearing completion by the time Susie and I left for our respective studies in the fall. It was beginning to look seaworthy, and Mama had agreed to make the sails. She rented an industrial sewing machine and began cutting and stitching great bolts of Dacron, with the same intensity she once applied to petticoats and pinafores. We watched in amazement, wondering what had become of our practical mother who had always preached against wasted hours and foolish fantasies.

"Do you think that boat of Daddy's will ever see the water?" I finally ventured.

"You never know . . . " she said evasively.

I returned from college the following summer to find that the project had been abandoned. A hornets' nest hung high astern. Mice and pigeons occupied the hull. But there were no regretful comments, and no explanations. Daddy had turned his attention to birdhouses again and to bicycle repair. He talked about getting himself in shape, maybe bicycling all the way around Lake Superior. Mama was helping him map out the route.

I gazed at the dry-docked vessel. At first I saw a big dream gone awry; later I knew I had failed to understand the voyage.

Daddy was tinkering with gears and spokes and humming as he worked. Mama was still milking her beloved herd of Holsteins. They had rigged the lifeboats and sailed in separate directions, avoiding ruinous storms and crippling doldrums. Each had steered a steady course through yet another year.

John

College. Freedom. Freedom from the milk and mud and manure of a dairy farm, from unrelenting work, and from the concern that I would never be able—or willing—to do my share. Freedom from my twin identity. No one comparing me to Susie, asking why I didn't play the piano. Freedom to be me.

I was shocked to find I didn't miss her more. Shocked and exhilarated. I could do this. I could make it on my own.

A disciplined and eager student, I earned A's in every class. I made friends easily; I liked and trusted everyone.

One October evening, walking alone from the university campus to downtown Eau Claire, I accepted a ride from two young men who cruised up beside me in a long, low Oldsmobile. They wanted me to sit between them in the front seat so we could get acquainted.

I learned that Dan and Terry were not fellow students, but garage mechanics, dressed in blue denim uniforms with their names stitched on the pockets. They must be nearly thirty, I decided. Dan wore a wedding ring. They offered to show me the town and the surrounding countryside. I said no thanks, I only wanted to go shopping—maybe another time—but we raced into the darkness. They kissed and petted me by turns; I was silent and compliant, ashamed, and yet afraid to spoil their fun.

"Please take me home now," I said politely. "It's getting late, and the dormitory will be locked at ten . . . "

"So the little virgins are locked up each night for safekeeping," Dan laughed, accelerating, showing no intention of turning back.

Now I sensed real danger and begged tearfully to be returned to Katherine Thomas Hall.

Dan pulled over to the side of the dark country road. Both men stepped out of the car and held a hasty conference while I cowered in the front seat, too frightened to cry.

They got back in the car and drove to the campus without speaking, letting me out a block from the dormitory. I raced for the door, greeted by the disapproving housemother who was turning her key in the lock.

I was lucky this time; safe for now.

Mama had often said, "Of all my kids, Sara is the most cooperative, the most *pliable*." She meant it as a compliment. Now I saw it as a stupid and precarious flaw.

Something was missing in me—something crucial to my independence, to my very safety and well being. I was not prepared to be a whole and healthy person, only the weaker half of a tightly bonded pair. I needed a partner to complete me, someone to guide me and protect me and tell me what I ought to do and think and feel.

I found him sitting next to me in freshman English. His name was John. He looked like a younger version of my father, with a crooked smile and a healthy crop of wavy brown hair.

John Drury's resemblance to my father ended with his physical appearance. He was self-assured—Mama might have said arrogant—a city boy raised in suburban Chicago. His family had recently moved to a sprawling lake home in southern Wisconsin where his father owned a food brokerage company. ("Another middle man!" Mama would later sneer. "No wonder the price of food is soaring out of sight—and the farmers aren't seeing a penny!")

During Christmas vacation, 1961, I visited the Drury home thirty miles west of Milwaukee on Upper Nemahbin Lake. The lake was long and elegant, like the modern homes that lined its shores. The evening meal (called dinner, rather than supper) was long and elegant as well. John, his mother and father, and three younger siblings spent more than an hour at the table each evening enjoying a five-course feast: garden salad; veal piccata, curried lamb, or chicken stewed in wine; crisp vegetables; dessert; a tray of fruit and cheese, followed by strong coffee and liqueur.

John's mother, who had all day to shop and prepare the gourmet meal, enjoyed rave reviews from every member of the family.

There was no rush to clear the table and scrape the plates, no pushing back of kitchen chairs, no frantic exit to the milking barn. They shared the highlights of the day with one another, then turned to national politics and world events.

"Do you think we're going to have a man on the moon during this decade, as John Kennedy predicts?"

"Of course we will!" John's father said.

"I don't think so," John debated. "The Mercury flights are an exciting step, but they're still suborbital—a long way from a lunar landing."

His father smiled respectfully. "You may be right. We'll see. It's a fascinating era for science and technology . . . "

"Let's take a trip to Cape Canaveral this year!"

Expansive conversations, high as the moon. No fretting about soggy fields or the market price of beef and milk and cheese. Every evening was a party, every weekend a vacation. This was a world that I could learn to love.

I began spending most of my free time with John, to the exclusion of my other friends. He liked to talk about his travels, and I listened eagerly. I had few adventures to report, and John did not seem to be curious about my homebound country life. I could hardly blame him. My farm stories would sound terribly boring to someone who had seen every corner of the United States, as well as Canada and Mexico.

Compared with my modest, introspective father, John was exciting, worldly, and bold. But apparently his boastful talk had not won him many college friends. He seemed lonely and needy in a way that I found quite compelling. By midwinter we felt firmly attached to each other. John began bringing his laundry and ironing to me, and he escorted me to breakfast, lunch, and dinner every day in the college dining hall.

We spent long hours walking hand in hand around the campus or cuddling and kissing in the dormitory lounge. Toward spring John suggested that it was time he met my family, and he offered to drive me home on Easter weekend. When I pointed out Polk County on the map, he laughed and teased. "Mud Lake. Horse Lake. Bone Lake. Luck. Milltown. I hope those places aren't as ugly as they sound."

"It's really very pretty county . . . "

"Never mind, Sweetheart. We won't be living there. A girl like you deserves a beautiful address."

I called Mama to warn her I might be bringing home a guest.

"That boy from Milwaukee? I don't know why you couldn't find someone closer to home. At least that way we'd have some notion of his background."

"He has a good background, Mama. I met his parents in December . . . "

"You had so many nice friends in high school. What's wrong with a hometown boy like Bobby Blattner? He was such a sweet young man. Remember when you and Susie and Bobby served as crown bearers back in second grade? You were just adorable together, marching across that gymnasium. I'll never understand why you turned him down that year he asked you to the Junior Prom."

I sighed. I might have known she would mention Bobby in an effort to burden me with pain and guilt.

"There was nothing wrong with Bobby, Mama. But he's dead, remember? He died in a car crash a few months after graduation."

"Of course I remember. I think about that grieving family nearly every day."

It was clear that Mama was not ready to accept my city boyfriend. I told John that Mama was not feeling good and delayed his visit until early summer.

John drove the 350 miles in his Volkswagen Beetle. Before he had even climbed out of the car Mama exclaimed, "Only nineteen years old, and he owns a vehicle! Does he have a job? He does? Well, then he ought to be saving all that money for his college education."

Daddy seemed to like John well enough and was pleased by his offer to help in the hayfield. Mama was not impressed, especially after John ignored her suggestion that he try on a pair of Daddy's Oshkosh overalls. He wore Bermuda shorts to load hay bales in the fresh-cut field; by evening his tanned legs were scratched and bleeding. Worse than that, he championed labor unions and daylight saving time, all in one disastrous conversation.

"Why is it, Helen, that farmers are so opposed to unionized labor?" he challenged as she thickened the stew.

While Mama was still preparing her defense, he raced on to a sorer subject.

"And why do farmers get upset about daylight saving time?"

She did not have to pause to answer that.

"Our work shouldn't have to suffer just because city folks with time to kill want to sit another hour in the sun!"

"What difference does it make to you? No matter how you slice it, there are just so many hours in the day."

"Farming runs according to the sun, not the clock, especially when someone has tinkered with the time. We can't get in the fields until the dew is off . . . "

Her voice sounded unnaturally sharp and high. I tried to signal John, but he persisted. "Forget the clock, then. Get up an hour later and work on standard time."

"What if we want to go to church or see a movie? We have to reckon with the outside world once in awhile. We have lives, too, you know!" She was nearly choking with exasperation.

John did not notice anything awry. He was accustomed to spirited debates at home. Minutes later he harassed her as she prepared the salad.

"My dad says lettuce leaves should be torn by hand, not cut—at least that's how it's done in better restaurants. Cutting causes the fragile leaves to bleed and wilt."

Mama pursed her lips and kept on chopping. When she attacked the celery with a butcher knife, John intervened—

"Oh, Helen! Stop! The celery heart is a delicacy—very nutritious—with an unusual flavor. It should never be discarded. If you don't mind I'll rescue this one from the garbage."

He fetched it out, trimmed it with a paring knife, salted it, and ate it with exaggerated pleasure as Mama looked on, flushed and speechless.

I knew where she wanted to plant that stalk of celery. I could see it in her eyes. No pampered college boy had the right to preach to her about thrift and waste—she who had scrimped and saved, feeding a large family and armies of ravenous threshers and harvest hands since long before he was born.

Nothing John could ever say would make up for that celery advice. I knew the visit was an utter failure; she could never be convinced to like him now.

Leaving Home

The following March I took the Greyhound bus from Eau Claire to Milltown. I had made the hundred-mile trip a dozen times during my two years at college, always looking forward to the weekend visit. Ted was sixteen already, strong and capable. Priscilla, at thirteen, was tall and serious and a willing helper in the barn. Both were good companions, eager to hear about my college life. But this time I was thinking of my parents. I had a difficult announcement for them, and I rehearsed it all the way home.

Mama and I cleaned up the supper dishes that evening at the kitchen sink. I washed. She dried. I still couldn't do dishes to her satisfaction, and we reverted to a familiar routine. If I didn't wash them well enough she slipped them back into the sudsy pond like undersized fish, without a word of reproach. She didn't need to fuss as long as she was making the final inspection.

"Just think, Sara," she said happily. "Nearly two years finished, two to go. Time flies so fast. Soon you'll be an English teacher like your Aunt Adele, independent, making an excellent wage."

It was time to break the news. "I have something to tell you," I began. "I won't be going back to school this fall."

Mama's mouth opened in protest, but I plunged ahead.

"I'll be having a baby."

Her mouth shut tight and hard. Then, "John is the father, I suppose."

"Yes. But we only did it once, Mama—honest," I pleaded, thinking it might somehow make a difference.

Bitter silence. She was wiping glasses furiously.

"I don't believe you. Anyway, that doesn't matter . . . one time or ten, you're just as pregnant, aren't you? Your father will be crushed. He had such hopes for you."

None of us knew what Daddy hoped for anymore, and I was furious whenever she spoke for him, interpreting his silences, using them as weapons against me.

"You mean *you're* heartbroken, don't you, Mama?"

"Well, we *both* expected . . . " She slammed a plate down on the tile counter top so hard that it shattered, then stooped to gather up the pieces.

"You're choosing poorly," she continued dully.

I did not feel that I was choosing at all—this thing was simply happening—but I was too proud to tell her that.

"I love him, Mama. He's a good person. You just refuse to trust anyone who isn't Scandinavian or doesn't know how to milk a cow!"

"I'm not as narrow-minded as you think," she said. "I just know that marriage can be plenty difficult, even when two people share similar backgrounds. And when your goals and expectations vary . . . "

"What do you even *know* about my goals, Mama?"

"Suppose you tell me, then. Just what do you want, young lady? And what kind of a life do you expect to have if you and John both lack a college education? There's obviously no farming in your future. You'll have to find some way to make a living. Have you considered that at all?"

I had considered it and found it frightening. But I had faith that we would manage somehow. If my parents had shown me anything, it was how to live with poor luck and hard times, how to tack on the lace and embroidery that would make them bearable.

She was not finished with me. "You had every chance your sisters did. Daddy and I would have sacrificed anything for you—you know that! Peggy has struggled through three years of nursing school, and Susie has worked so hard to become a first-rate pianist. And *you*—you throw away your future."

Her voice cracked. "I have always been careful not to compare you twins, but I don't understand why you've been satisfied to stay in the background, second best. You have the same talents, the same potential as your sister. If you don't care about yourself, you might at least think of your father and me and all we've sacrificed for you!" She was crying now. "You know I can't stand waste of any kind!"

I wanted to stop her. I was tempted to describe my frantic state of mind when I walked from the doctor's office back to campus one week earlier. I had come close to marching straight into the rushing traffic. Pregnant. A baby. No more college. Marriage, when I knew both John and I were so unready. How could we ever make this work? And how could I explain it to Mama? For a wild moment death had seemed preferable to the angry words that I knew she would fling at me.

"Mama," I began defensively, "this isn't the way I planned it either, but John and I will be all right. Maybe I can go back to school later. It's not the end of everything."

"It's the end," she said.

"Is it such a waste, Mama, to marry and raise children?"

Her eyes were like green stones.

"You'll understand when you're as used up and bone tired as I am."

"Oh, Mama, is that really how you feel?"

She couldn't stop. "Pretty soon you'll be as thick as a tree. I guess you won't feel quite so sassy then."

I rushed out in my thin sweater, unaware of the cold, drawn to the sturdy oak that stood beside the barn. Daddy's old tire swing was swaying from the lowest limb. I eased inside its cradling arms and rocked against the wind.

Mama rallied, of course.

"Daddy is in bed today," she said evenly the next morning at the breakfast table. "He has a nasty cold, and I'm afraid he's also feeling quite depressed. It seems to hit him every spring about this time, just when we're faced with all this plowing and seeding. Luckily Ted and I can almost manage this place without him."

I realized we had ridden the peaks of Daddy's temper and the troughs of his depressions for so long that they seemed normal and expected, like the turning seasons. Now I voiced a nagging question: "Don't you think that we've pretended for too long that everything is fine? Maybe if we'd found some counseling—or forced him into some decision . . . "

"I think he's done all right, under the circumstances."

"But they were lousy circumstances for a man who hated dairy farming. Maybe if he'd stayed with sheep—or tried some different occupation . . . "

"Times were tough. His choices have been pretty limited."

"I suppose so . . . "

"Wait till you become a parent. You'll learn about restrictions then, I promise you. And you're not ready for them—that's what hurts so much."

"We weren't talking about me, Mama."

"Well, I think we ought to be."

I gave up then; I could think of nothing more to say.

"Don't worry about your father," she consoled me. "He'll feel better in a week or two, then he'll start nailing up some birdhouses or tinkering with a bicycle. I'm going out to finish up the chores. Go on in and talk to him before you have to leave."

I tapped on the bedroom door. No response. Quietly I entered and approached the bed. Daddy lay on his back, eyes roving over the ceiling. When he finally glanced uncomfortably at me, I knew Mama had shared my news and felt glad I didn't have to tell it myself.

"I'm sorry you're sick, Daddy. I wish I didn't have to go so soon, but the bus leaves at eleven. Don't worry about me now, I'll be just fine."

"I know."

He wore a slight, lopsided smile. I had never learned to read that vague expression—it could mean anything from mild amusement to deep despair. This time I saw a faint dismissal; he wanted me to disappear so he could think about his own mistakes.

I thought he must be grieving for a life of passive choices, for murmuring yes when he had wanted to shout no. For misdirected bolts of temper, followed by guilty silence. For wanting too much, accepting too little. For gazing after trains he should have risked his life to leap aboard. Grieving for a daughter who had watched and learned too well.

In June I took a train myself, bound for Biloxi, Mississippi, to join my husband who had enlisted in the air force. It was John's plan, and it made sense to me. Uncle Sam would pay for the baby's birth. We could be independent, make a new start far away from both our families.

Susie was in summer school at the University of Wisconsin in Madison, and our good-byes were in the mail. I dreaded the farewells yet to come.

Daddy made a final inspection of the sturdy wooden trunk he had constructed, checking to be sure the hinges were fast, the lock secure. Inside the trunk were four perfect, matching dinner plates, cups, and saucers, assorted pots and utensils, embroidered tea towels and pillow slips, clean patched bed linens, and a Holy Bible. Mama had packed her Sunday best for me.

"You'll be needing some respectable dinnerware, so I picked out the best I could find. Cracked dishes are good enough for service on the farm. Busy men never stay at the table long enough to study an empty plate," she chattered. "I put in four of everything—you always had a knack for making friends, and you'll be wanting to entertain . . . "

"I'll miss you, Mama."

"We'll miss you, too."

Her nose was red. Her eyes filled up behind the heavy glasses. We hadn't hugged in years and surely couldn't start now. Mama said she had to hurry to the barn—she was doctoring one cow for mastitis and another was down with a mysterious fever. She guessed it might be time to call the vet. I shouldn't bother to come out. The barn smell had a way of clinging to the hair and clothes . . .

Daddy was unusually talkative when he took me to meet the train. The Soo Line no longer served our little town, nor any towns nearby. We had to drive all the way to the Union Depot in St. Paul.

"I envy you, really, going off on the train to a new place," he said. "I wanted to hop the train every time I saw it roll out of the Milltown depot. Just ride the rails, you know, find out where they might lead. But I got myself stuck with those damned Holsteins. I was never much of a farmer, always felt like a square peg in a round hole. Just couldn't keep up with Mama and Grandpa Willie and the boys—and wasn't sure I wanted to. What's so damned wonderful about working yourself to death that way? Is that really what life is all about?"

I said I didn't think so.

"I should have been a naturalist, or a forest ranger. Figured that out too late, of course, after I got stuck with farming. Well, farming wasn't all bad, not in the early days," Daddy continued. "By God, I knew how to get along with a team of horses. And I sure could manage a flock of sheep. Now cows are another story. Cows and tractors. They're about equally useless inventions to my way of thinking. But Mama wanted to go into Holsteins. And hell—from a practical standpoint, she was right. This is cow country. It looks as if dairying is the only way a farmer can make any money in this neck of the woods. But once I got tied down with a big herd of cattle and all that costly machinery, I was finished. . . . Maybe if I'd gone into railroading, like my dad. Nah, the railroads are folding, too. I just don't know. I suppose I was born in the wrong century. What does a fellow do about that, anyway?"

The train was pulling into view. Daddy squeezed my arm and leaned forward with his familiar lopsided smile.

"I don't suppose Mama ever mentioned this, but your Grandma and Grandpa Williamson got married a bit—ah—prematurely, too."

I looked up in genuine surprise. He reddened.

"As they say, it can happen in the best of families. And ours is one of the best, in spite of some bad timing here and there. Now don't let on to your mother that I told that little secret. She has a lot of family pride, and that's a good thing, really."

The whistle called.

"You're going to make a fine mother, too. We'll be thrilled about the baby, and very proud of you."

I hugged him quickly and climbed aboard, taking a seat at the nearest window, wiping it clear with my gloved hand. I watched and waved until the moving train had shrunk him to a tiny peg upon the platform, then rolled him out of sight.

Epilogue

In our college days, Susie and I came home bringing our disturbing doubts and liberal philosophies along like laundry. Dirty clothes and tainted notions would be dashed and wrung and hung out clean by our efficient mother.

We spoke of hedonism and "free love."

"Love isn't *free*," said Mama.

We rued our puritanical upbringing and spoke about the need to "find ourselves."

"I'll never understand this nonsense the young people are spouting. Why do you need to *find yourselves* anyway? Why are you lost? Life is so simple. Work hard. Be kind to your neighbors. What more do you need to know?"

Made wise by introductory courses in psychology and social science, I saw my mother as hopelessly rigid, my father as a tragic hero, who had railed all his adult life against the bitter boundaries of his ill-chosen work.

I felt determined not to fall into those traps. I would not settle for a cramped, country existence. I would write letters home from far-flung places. I would marry a man like my father, who yearned for travel and adventure but had the confidence to carry out his dreams.

During my marriage to John Drury, we lived in Biloxi, Mississippi (where our first son was born); in Fort Worth, Texas; East Lansing, Michigan; Milwaukee, Wisconsin; and Queensland, Australia. When John, seven-year-old Billy, and I left for Australia in 1970, John declared that the move was permanent and irreversible. We would transport only what Qantas Airlines would allow and dispose of the rest, leaving nothing to come back to in the U.S.A. We were immigrants. No looking back. That attitude would be essential to our success in an adopted land.

Although both John and I found employment and soon owned a modern home in suburban Brisbane, I failed completely as an immigrant. Unlike my great-grandparents, who had sailed from their native Norway a century earlier, I was aware that I had choices. I could fly home in a single day if the reasons were compelling. Adapting was not critical to my survival. I could afford to mourn.

And mourn I did. I longed to see snowdrifts, spring violets, white birches and blazing sugar maples, red timber barns anchored by concrete silos, Holstein cattle dotting the Wisconsin countryside. I deplored the Aussie's twisted vowels and craved the sing-song speech of mid-America. I missed my parents and siblings so much that my stomach ached. When my marriage ended in December 1973, I brought two sons—one-year-old Michael and ten-year-old Billy—back to the family farm.

It was a temporary refuge. I had come home just as my father was struggling to make his great escape. "Forty-four years of farming. I think I've done my time," he said, sounding more defeated than determined.

My brother, Teddy, helped him to get free, proposing that they sell the farm to him. He'd milk another year or two if prices held, but his long-term plan involved cash cropping and maybe some beef cattle, combined with a machine-shop business.

Mama resisted at first, but when a choice was pressed on her, she valued her husband's health more than a herd of cows. She must have known, too, that the small farm faced a precarious future. Half of the 5.5 million farms operating in 1950 had been consolidated out of existence by 1974. The average size of the American farm had doubled in that time; machinery costs had trebled. The shrinking profit margin meant a farmer had to milk more cows, acquire more land, equipment, and machines, and carry a debt load he could support only through further expansion. The choice was simple. Grow or die.

In April 1975, their seventy head of top-grade milk cows and heifers were sold at auction, and my parents moved to town.

Leaving the farm was wrenching for Mama. She continued to rise at dawn and filled her empty days creating oddities. We all received several brightly painted stone ladybugs that, too large for their magnetized mountings, crawled down our refrigerators and plopped on the floor. Next came roadrunner puppets, crafted from drapery cord, Styrofoam balls, fake feathers, and clomping jar-lid feet.

One day I found Mama sitting at her kitchen table, staring blankly at a flock of freshly glued roadrunners.

"Ever since I left the farm I feel so *purposeless*," she said, as close to tears as I had ever seen her. "That was such big, important work. Now I'm as useless as these silly puppets."

I worried needlessly. Within a year Mama found engrossing projects with the local historical society and was also in demand as an accompanist, church organist, grandmother, helpful friend, and neighbor.

Daddy retired with gusto. He built enough birdhouses to shelter all the bluebirds in Polk County. In 1975 he bought a flea-market bicycle for thirty dollars, began tinkering with it, and later that summer took to the open road. He felt in harmony with his machine. It was quiet. Efficient and uncomplicated. The summer of 1976 he led a Bikecentennial tour from Astoria, Oregon, to Yorktown, Virginia, covering 4,450 miles. Over the next ten years he toured thirty states and three Canadian provinces, logging over fifteen thousand miles.

Mama and Daddy also bought a travel trailer and saw North America together, as well as touring England, Scotland, Wales, Australia, and New Zealand.

During the years our parents were traveling extensively and enjoying their well-earned freedom, my sisters and I were searching for stability. Peggy earned a nursing degree and married a physician. They made their home in Massachusetts and had a son and daughter. After college Priscilla returned to Polk County to raise a family and serve as organist in her hometown church. Susie pursued her career as a piano teacher and performing artist in Minneapolis. I became a medical secretary, more by default than by design, and lived in numerous cities. But while my twin and I were widely separated by locations and life-styles, in some respects our lives ran parallel. We married, divorced, and remarried within months of each other. And through it all we kept our telepathic contact, often hearing busy signals on the phone because we were dialing each other at the same time.

In 1984 my new husband—whom I had met and married in Florida—suggested that we move to Polk County, which he declared the most peaceful place that he had ever seen. We drove up north for an extended visit and made the decision to move. The countryside had not changed much since the 1950s, except for some collapsing dairy barns and empty silos. A few new houses were appearing here and there, occupied by urban commuters. I saw unique, enduring beauty. A place that would invite me to reflect and remember. And write.

"*Dancing the Cows Home*. That's a curious title," my sons said when I mentioned my writing project. They had both been traveling—conducting courtships and educational and business ventures in Europe, South America, Africa, and China.

"What's the book about?"

My responses were brief because I had an old-fashioned respect for the long-distance cable that I still imagined jumping and twitching on the ocean floor. And possibly because I wasn't sure of my purpose.

"It's about cows. And dancing."

"No, really. What are you writing about? And why?"

I wondered that, too.

I told my sons I was writing about change. And stability.

A personal past; a shared future. The great continuum.

Finding roots; getting free.

Pressed further, I said I was writing about my mother and her appetite for work, my siblings and their craving for beauty and perfection, my father and his need to know the world that stretched beyond his fence line. And I was trying to climb back inside those fences to a time and place that felt like home.